The Healing Power of Love

THE HEALING POWER OF LOVE

BRAD STEIGER

1469 Morstein Road
West Chester, Pennsylvania 19380 USA

The Healing Power of Love

International Standard Book Number: 0-914918-84-2
Library of Congress Catalog Card Number: 88-50420

Edited by Skye Alexander
Cover design by Bob Boeberitz

Published by Whitford Press
A division of Schiffer Publishing, Ltd.

This book may be purchased from the publisher.
Please include $2.00 postage.
Try your bookstore first.
Please send for free catalog to:
Whitford Press
c/o Schiffer Publishing, Ltd.
1469 Morstein Road
West Chester, Pennsylvania 19380

Manufactured in the United States of America

Contents

1

The Greatest Power in the Universe

"And now abide faith, hope, and love, these three: but the greatest of these is love." *St. Paul*

For many years I have featured a segment on healing in each of my seminars. I do not present myself as a faith healer, but through a focus on love, the greatest power in the universe, I have been privileged to serve as the channel for some remarkable healings.

After one of my recent appearances in Los Angeles, the mail brought me the following testimonials to the healing power of love:

From a victim of Multiple Sclerosis who had been confined to a wheelchair: "Here is a picture of me at my darlin' daughter's wedding. I'm *standing*, and I *walked* down the aisle to start the wedding. And it is all due to the magnificent healing that you projected. I can never thank you adequately enough. If it hadn't been for the healing, I would have been stuck in a chair as an observer and missed being a part of my daughter's wedding."

From a woman diagnosed as having ovarian cysts: "My first meeting with you was through your many informative and inspiring books. During [the seminar] I accepted your offer of healing. I felt very much in need, as I had been diagnosed as having ovarian cysts by three medical doctors, confirmed by a sonogram. The doctor recommended exploratory surgery to determine whether or not the cysts were malignant. I had decided not to undergo surgery. After the healing session, I had a follow-up sonogram—which showed no cysts present. I can only attribute the disappearance of the cysts to your healing. God bless you in your enlightened work."

Love Is An Image of God

As I always stress in my seminars, I, of myself, can do nothing. But if I open myself properly to the Love Force that flows from the heart of the universe, healing miracles can be manifested through the exercises and techniques that I share with my audiences. I wish to offer a number of these processes to you.

Since, as Goethe said, we are shaped and fashioned by what we love, then it certainly behooves us to hold the highest ideal of love in our hearts and minds at all times. The essence of that ideal should be our concept of God. And since, as the scripture writer declares, "God is love," then so, too, is love the energy that is most god-expressive.

"Love is an image of God, and not a lifeless image, but the living essence of the divine nature which beams full of all goodness," stated the great theologian Martin Luther.

There is no question that effort is necessary to maintain the discipline that is required to make us pure and effective vehicles for the healing power of love. Balance of ego, spirit, and body must be realized, and the energy of the dark side of the Love Force must be avoided.

To serve as a conduit for the healing energy, one must open the spiritual centers as wide as possible. And there have been times, due to the demands of the moment—or to my over-confidence—that I did not provide adequate protection for my own psyche. At the same time, to meet a growing demand for my services, I began to emphasize the mechanics of healing more than the power of love.

I stood on the speaker's platform articulate, effective, stimulating. But while I may have been helping others, I was not serving myself. I was in the lamentable position that the epistle writer Paul describes: "Though I speak with the tongues of men and of angels and have not love in my heart, I am become as a sounding brass or a tinkling cymbal. And though I have the gift of prophecy and understand all mysteries and all knowledge; and though I have all faith so that I could remove mountains and have not love in my heart, I am nothing."

During a darkened period of my life, I saw my quest as a kind of extended allegory paralleling the parable of the sower and the seeds. I saw how Soul-seeds, blessed by light and love, are scattered by strong, eternal hands—some to grow in friendly earth, some to die on unyielding stone. However, not all those pitiful dying seeds fall on rocky ground or into the grasp of throttling weeds. Some, alas, find fertile soil, but then they defiantly expose themselves to hostile elements, as if to dare the dark forces to halt their growth.

I saw myself as such a foolhardy seedling. My roots had been strong, my reaching branches firm; but my zeal had permitted my spirit to become enveloped by an evil blight that had come from far beyond the parameters of my arrogance, far beyond my power to endure. I had dared to walk where angels feared to tread; and in my reckless confidence, I had believed that I could emerge from such expeditions unscathed.

As my spiritual energy began to yield to depression and uncertainty, my family and friends became concerned that this "seedling" might truly begin to wither and surrender its life force to chaos.

My Own Testimony to Love's Healing Power

As a "seed" that had experienced a sad halting of the spiritual growth process, I was blessed by the meeting of a most compassionate gardener, Sherry Hansen, a licensed and ordained Protestant minister, an accomplished crisis counselor, a skilled healer, and one of the founding members of the Holistic Healing Board through the Institutes of Health and Education, Washington, D.C. By blending her destiny with my own, Sherry has brought me back on course and has chosen to walk beside me through life's challenges and opportunities, supporting me with her love, her encouragement, and her example. Sherry is one who has elected to live as an expression of the power of love to heal.

As a once-blighted seed, I can now affirm that we must have the abiding love of one another and the eternal love of the God-Force, and I offer my own psalm of thanksgiving:

There will only be darkness unless someone who cares brings new light to straighten the twisted branches.

There will only be everlasting thirst unless a loving water bearer brings the liquid of life to rejuvenate the parched roots.

When a dying seed is brought back to life, a miracle has been wrought.

I was such a seed.
You are my miracle.
I love you, O Caretaker of my Soul.

Integral to the exercises and techniques of healing that I share in this book is the following truism that was expressed by Jean Paul Richter: "Love one human being purely and warmly, and you will love all."

While the healing of the body is a noble goal and brings us comfort, let us remember that a healthy soul brings us peace—and that neither is possible without love.

"Love is the greatest thing that God can give us," observed Jeremy Taylor, "for He, himself, is love. And love is the greatest thing that we can give to God, for it will also give of ourselves and carry with it all that is ours. The apostle calls Love the bond of perfection; it is the old, the new, the great commandment and all the commandments, for it is the fulfilling of the law."

The Pyramid of Love Exercise

This process becomes a kind of universal blessing of unconditional love which you can transmit to the world.

Visualize a beautiful golden pyramid manifesting directly above your head, immediately above your crown chakra. Understand that this pyramid is filled with love from the Source of All-That-Is. Feel this great love from the very center of the Cosmos beaming down into your crown chakra.

And now sense the warmth of the universal love moving down from your crown chakra into your chest, your heart chakra. Feel that love blending with your own and streaming out of your heart chakra to touch the heart of another being. Know that you have made a positive love connection with another. Focus upon someone near you and know that you have touched that person with love.

Understand clearly that the more love that you issue forth from your heart chakra, the more love will stream down into your crown chakra from the Golden Pyramid of Love with its Crystal Capstone of pure love energy from the Source. The more love you transmit, the more love will be poured into you from the Golden Pyramid directly above your crown chakra.

And now visualize a dear one who needs healing. Picture your love like a golden cord unwinding from your heart chakra and making a positive connection with this loved one who needs the healing energy. See this person responding to your love connection.

Visualize someone who is lonely, fearful of life. Touch that person with your love. Let that person know that somewhere there is one who cares, who transmits love.

See your love traveling around the world, touching those who need love, connecting with those who need to feel that they are not alone.

And once the great circle has been completed, see that your love has orbited back to the Golden Pyramid above your crown chakra, once again filling you with love from the Source of All-That-Is, from the very center of the Universe.

2

The Healing Energy of Love

The emphatic words of the young doctor with the penetrating eyes and compelling voice were directed to the young woman in the isolation ward of the city hospital. She had been given only three weeks to live. Tuberculosis was eating her lungs and her life away.

The woman stirred feebly, moving almost as if the sputtering spark of life had suddenly received a fresh breath of air.

"I have received permission to take you to your home," the young doctor said softly, not telling her that the hospital had thought it a kindness to let her die in her home. "There I will call on you. Together we will work to make you well."

The woman blinked her eyes in wonder at the young man's unbelievable reassurance. Could he be serious? She was dying! Still there was something about his manner...

Thirty years later, the woman who had had her death certificate on a doctor's desk waiting to be signed was a beautiful matron who suffered no major physical difficulties since her healing. One of her closest friends was Dr. Cushing Smith of Detroit, Michigan, no longer a young man, but still devoted to helping his fellow man, still healing those who lie in beds of suffering.

Attacking Illness through Right Thinking

Dr. Smith believes—along with many modern scientists—that the cause of all illness lies within our own mental habits, our relation to others and, ultimately, to God. Therefore, our health should be within our own grasp, and illness should be attacked successfully through understanding proper prayer and right thinking.

"The thing that differentiates my work from that of a psychiatrist," explains Dr. Smith, "is that I do not confine my investigation to the consciousness or subconsciousness of the individual. I recognize the fact that many diseases originate in the mentalities of *others* whose thoughts are directed at the patient.

"The psychiatrist can do nothing about prenatal influences, pre-incarnation and mental malpractice which enter into many cases of disease and suffering."

Dr. Smith feels that the metaphysics of the body was better understood in ancient times than today. He notes, however, that the current investigation of psychosomatic medicine might once again point out the mental significance of disease.

"Operations, drugs, injections only put the patient on probation until he completely destroys the errors which threw his body out of balance in the first place," Dr. Smith says.

Mental therapy based on metaphysical etiology must be understood, according to Dr. Smith. "Recognition of this fact will enable the patient to work with the doctor and with such cooperation medicine will have a double-barreled effect."

The Symbolic Names of the Anatomy

Dr. Smith explains that the names given to various parts of the body are symbolic, and that a clear understanding of the "metaphysics of anatomy" is essential to effective healing.

For example, in his book *I Can Heal Myself, and I Will,*

he interprets the ribs as essentially designed for the protection of the internal organs. They signify a breastwork, or fortress, that protects against the sword thrusts of hatred and evil thought. Broken ribs and injuries to the chest are to be approached from this viewpoint.

Leg bones, as seen metaphysically, signify support, financial, moral, civic or ethical. Therefore, a broken leg is not adequately healed until some attention is paid to its mental significance and the appropriate metaphysical remedy is administered.

Acknowledge that God is Love

"Before one can be healed or heal others, he must acknowledge that God is Love," Dr. Smith says. "He must be determined to look for love in everyone that he meets, in spite of the obvious appearance to the contrary. One must approach healing with humility, sincerity and depth of understanding."

"I always begin by attacking fear," Dr. Smith explains. "Fear is an element of every disease, that tends to keep the patient in bondage."

Healing is seldom instantaneous and it may take a year or more to achieve victory.

"It is often plain that so-called incurable ailments lie deep in the subconscious, perhaps placed there by the mental reactions of the patient's mother during pregnancy. Such cases require patient metaphysical digging," comments Dr. Smith.

For example, in the healing of a brain tumor Dr. Smith discovered that the growth was the physical manifestation of the patient's colossal egotism and his desire to be a good fellow. His mother's prenatal conviction that he would be twins was the predisposing cause.

Says Dr. Smith, "No better prescription for overcoming fear exists than the Biblical pronouncement: 'There is no fear in Love!'"

"Love is the purification of heart from self; it strengthens and ennobles the character, gives a higher motive and a nobler aim to every action of life, and makes both man and woman strong, noble, and courageous; the power to love truly and devotedly is the noblest gift with which a human being can be endowed; but it is a sacred fire that must not be burned to idols."

Maria Jane Jewsbury

Using the Golden Circle to Heal

"In its simplest form, the Golden Circle is really the concentration of the power of your mind, body, and soul in a radiant, dynamic circle about your body," the great seer and clairvoyant Dorothy Spence Lauer told me. "You will soon discover that it is the force in back of your life; it is the invisible, magnetic power that flows in the universe, which man may channel with his mind and release in a dynamic stream of radiant energy. Yet it is more, ever so much more! It is actually a potent power of God's infinite intelligence as it animates all creation."

According to Dorothy:

"The Golden Magic Circle will make you a much different person. Every atom and cell of your brain will become charged with positive thoughts.

There are those afflicted with cancer who are worried and say that they know someone put a curse on them. The first thing I tell this person is that he must first of all, with all his heart, say, 'I now place (name of person) lovingly in the hands of the Father. That which is for his own highest good shall come to him.'

Then, of course, one cannot turn around and add a lot of things that he would like to have happen to the person. If someone has hurt you, cursed you, or caused you any unhappiness in life, you must leave it directly in the Father's hands."

Cancer Victims and Grudge-Bearing

I believe that in time scientists will discover, as I have, that many cancer victims have harbored a grudge of long standing against another person.

One, whom I knew, was a woman who detested her daughter-in-law. I asked her one day, after the daughter-in-law had left, why she felt so antagonistic toward this young woman. She told me it was because she felt the woman had taken her son from her. The daughter-in-law was a wonderful wife and mother, and I am afraid I was not too sympathetic with the mother-in-law.

The mother-in-law was a very religious woman, and she became quite irritated with me when I told her that until she released this animosity toward her daughter-in-law, there would be no chance of her ever recovering from cancer. She was so angry that she did not talk to me for about two weeks.

Then she became very ill. She called me and told me that I had been right, but she had been too stubborn to admit it. She said that her son's wife was not the person that she had wanted him to marry, and she had nurtured a grudge within her. If the young woman was nice to her, she accused her of having an ulterior motive. If she stood up for her rights, then the mother told her son that his wife was treating her cruelly.

Another very dear friend of mine had also developed cancer. I told her frankly that she must have some begrudging thought in her mind about someone. Usually people get very angry when I tell them this, and if you who are reading this happen to have cancer, you may be angry, too. But until you get that thought out of your mind, you are actually helping that cancer eat away the very tissues of your body. You are literally eating yourself up with anger.

This friend of mine finally admitted that she was very angry with her mother, because her mother had been so unreasonable with her all of her life. Instead of expressing her displeasure, she had kept this inside of her. I begged her to talk to her mother without, of course, being disrespectful. I urged her to explain to her mother the feeling that she had held within her all these years.

My friend did talk to her mother, then went ahead with a cancer operation. Today she is well and happy, and she has said that since she released the hatred from her mind, she and her mother are very dear to each other. Her mother told her that she had not meant to be cruel, she simply felt that she had done the right thing at that particular time.

I have talked to many, many people who have had cancer, and in each and every case, the person has admitted that he or she nurtured a grudge against someone. I am convinced that if we harbor hatred, it becomes a corrosive, self-consuming acid.

Change Your Reality with God's Golden Circle

Once you have put the Golden Magic Circle around you, you will feel entirely different than you have felt before. You will almost sense a "presence." Things that once bothered you and caused you to be very concerned suddenly will not be quite as important as they were before you had the Golden Magic Circle around you. Don't be surprised if people notice a change in your personality.

Your dynamic thought atmosphere will be radiant. You will possess a certain magnetism and graciousness. There will be a pronounced air of truth, goodness, and peace that you have never noticed before. You can select anything you want in this life. If you just visualize what you want-and fix it firmly enough in your mind, it will come to pass. Keep this in mind as you draw your Golden Magic Circle around you.

To make your Golden Magic Circle, visualize a golden circle—quite a large one—completely surrounding you. This alone brings you much good. This circle will never leave you. If you happen to be in danger, upset, or discouraged, you should just remember that your Magic Circle is completely surrounding you. Since this Magic Circle is of God, you know it is good.

The moment you have pictured your Golden Magic Circle around your body, spread your arms and visualize that area as being completely filled with golden light, your own mental and spiritual kingdom. You can now be queen or king in this particular area, as you become oriented to this Magic Circle.

Visualize now a golden line of infinity, going from the top of your head to God, as your lifeline goes to God as a source of supply, rather than to the world.

Visualize this lifeline holding you aloft when you are tired or feeling discouraged. You will instantly notice that your head goes up, your spine stiffens. You will be erect so long as the Magic Circle cord is tight.

Now visualize another line going from your diaphragm, or waist, to the horizon. This is the other lifeline which ties you to God's infinity.

As you breathe deeply of the golden elixir that surrounds you in your Magic Circle, you will be sustained and supported. You may feel at this moment that His presence is all around you. You will never feel alone again, because always beside you in your own Magic Circle is this invisible presence of God. You will know that things will be different from this moment on.

Whenever you are upset, give a little tug to your lifeline, and you will receive help almost instantly, or something will come to you that will tell you what to do and what to say in this particular instance. Opportunities may present themselves at this time which will be very astonishing to you. You should let the energy of your soul rise above petty annoyances, as they can only affect the physical you: they can never destroy the immortal, or divine, part of you which is your soul.

Troubles may arise and you may become upset and tempted to let go. That is the time to pull upon the invisible cord which ties you to God's line, to raise your thoughts, to lift up your eyes to Heaven and, instead of being limited to this Earth's horizon, breathe deeply and inhale the breath of God.

A baby cries out and proclaims its entrance into the world. This infusion of the breath of life is God's Magic Circle. A child has faith in its parents. This is the kind of child-like faith you must have in God. You should feel that your hand is placed in His, and then you can fear no evil.

"Prayer is the wing wherewith the soul flies to heaven. Meditation is the eye where with we see God." *St. Ambrose*

3

The Perfect You

You can focus the healing power of love to enable you to create any positive physical condition that you wish. If you can make a commitment to practice the following exercise on a regular basis, you will quickly begin to shape the perfect you.

Sit quietly in a place where you will be undisturbed by all external stimuli for at least thirty minutes. Calm yourself and attempt to clear your mind of all troublesome thoughts.

Take a comfortably deep breath, hold it for the count of three, then exhale slowly.

Take another comfortably deep breath, hold it for the count of four, exhale slowly.

Then take a third comfortably deep breath, hold it for the count of five, exhale very slowly.

Accept that you have within you a Higher Self that is the ultimate you. This Higher Self is a magnificent blueprint of your perfect self, the very image of that which you have the potential to become.

Form a mental picture of yourself as your Higher Self. See yourself exactly as you know you have the potential to become. Hold the image of your Higher Self in your mind.

The mental picture of your perfect self must make *no* reference to the way that you *now* appear. You must only focus on your perfect self as you wish yourself to be. You must *not* visualize at any time your body condition as it is at the present.

If you send a thought form to your Higher Self which includes a mental "photograph" of your illness, it is as if you are sending "before" and "after" pictures. The result will be muddled.

You must believe that within your Higher Self is the true image of your perfect self. And you must hold in your mind the thought of how you envision your perfect self to be.

Once you have fashioned that image of your perfect physical self, hold it fast and begin to breathe in very slowly, taking comfortably deep breaths. As you inhale, you are drawing in what some mystics refer to as the *mana*, and what martial artists refer to as the *ki* or the *chi*, the all-pervasive life force. The same unknown energy that permits them to smash boards with their bare hands or walk on hot coals will also allow you to shape the physical condition of your choice.

Make and memorize the picture of your perfect self as you breathe and draw in the *mana*. The mana will give the picture enough strength to hold together while the High Self begins to materialize the image into physical actuality.

Hold the picture firmly in your mind as you continue to breathe slowly, sending energy to the Higher Self.

Live in the picture.

Feel it.

Keep your mind from all negative thought to the contrary.

Visualizing the Perfect You

You may read the following visualization, pausing now and then to reflect upon the process. Or, you may wish to have a friend read the techniques to you as you relax and experience the imagery. It is also possible to record your own voice, reading this exercise into a tape recorder, so that you can play the tape back and allow your own voice to guide you through the relaxation process and the procedure.

Any of the above methods can be effective. Just be certain when you do this that you will not be disturbed for at least thirty minutes. As an additional aid to the process, you might play some inspirational background music to heighten the effect. Be certain, though, that the music contains no lyrics to distract you.

Your success in this exercise depends upon your willingness to permit a transformation to manifest in your consciousness.

The Floating Cloud Technique

Permit yourself to relax...totally and completely. Lie back in a comfortable position and release all worries...all tensions...all problems. Let your mind float. Relax...relax.

Take three comfortably deep breaths and relax.

Now imagine before you the softest, fluffiest cloud in the sky.

See it settling down next to you as you relax...relax.

See yourself crawling upon it to rest...to float...to relax...to rise to the sky and leave all your problems behind you...leave all your tensions behind you.

Float and drift, drift and float, rising to the sky in a comfortable slow, swinging motion. Nothing will disturb you. Nothing will distress you. No sound will bother you. In fact, should you hear any sound at all, that sound will only help you to relax.

Take three more comfortably deep breaths...and relax.

You are floating up into the sky, drifting higher and higher. You feel safe and totally secure. It is impossible for you to fall.

Feel peace and contentment. Drift...and float. Drift and float. You are entering a feeling of total peace and total relaxation.

As you are drifting and floating with your mind completely at peace, you are aware that your body has been rising higher and higher. You have been comfortably soaring through the clouds, and the higher you float, the less you are aware of any stress or tension. All of your body is completely relaxed. Your toes...feet...legs...torso...arms...shoulders...neck...all are totally relaxed.

Now you are aware of a great bolt of electrical energy that is shooting toward you. You know that it will not harm you in any way. In fact, it will energize you. It will energize you and give you strength and love. It will give you the power to mold and shape your body any way that you most desire it to be.

Feel the soothing, yet exhilarating, warmth as this bolt of power touches your body. Feel the warm, tingling love energy moving throughout your entire body. Feel the love energy moving down your spine, bringing great strength and power to your entire being. Feel the love energy gathering in your arms, your back, your chest, your legs.

You are now aware of another great bolt of electrical energy shooting toward you. It is another Lightning Bolt of Strength and Love. You feel its warm energy touching you. Two powerful surges of energy course through your body, and you are aware of great strength building in each of your muscles.

And now a third Lightning Bolt of Strength and Love touches and activates you with incredible energy. You can feel a mounting surge of power multiplying within your body. You are pulsating with power and energy.

You are surging with power such as you have never before experienced.

You will be stronger and healthier than you have ever been. You will give full expression to the Lightning Bolt of Strength and Love. You feel energy rhythmically pulsating deep within your being, your very essence.

See your body shaping itself, molding itself, to the image that you fashion within your mind. You will see every muscle in your body responding to your will.

Each and every cell within your body will obey your commands to shape, to mold, to sculpt themselves as you envision them. Each and every cell within your body will obey your mental commands to shape, to mold, to sculpt precisely the physical condition of health that you most desire.

At the count of three, you will emerge from this state of relaxation feeling better than you have felt in weeks and weeks.

ONE...eager to continue to shape your body as you wish it.

TWO...each cell, fiber, and muscle ready to be molded and shaped.

THREE...charged with the Lightning Bolt of Strength and Love...Healthy as never before!

AWAKEN!

4

Love is the Greatest Healer

My friend Bryce Bond of New York City is one of the most remarkable spiritual healers I have ever known. In the following chapter, he shares some of his most intimate feelings concerning the healing power of love:

I feel very close to God, in a spiritual way. I believe that God is in every man, woman, and child. He is life itself.

Then I watch how the world seems to close in on certain individuals, and how they let the self-imposed limitations surround them into illness.

Many people realize that a disease is nothing more than a disharmony within themselves. A disharmony of body, mind and spirit. Many of the problems we have today are of a psychosomatic origin. We have to treat the cause of the effect, and then after we find the cause, the effect is quite often healed.

We allow ourselves to think that we are in total control of our own lives. Our egos become enlarged, neglecting our higher selves, our spirits. This creates a gap between us and God.

I believe that God does the healing. I can do nothing. I am only a channel for God's healing power.

I don't want to sound overly religious, for I'm not. I do not agree with the teachings of orthodox religions. Yet it is needed as a balance between the physical and mental.

I think that when we begin to hold onto fears, anger, hate, resentment, envy, frustration and all the other negative emotions, we bring about our own sicknesses—sicknesses within, manifesting into the physical.

There must be millions of ways to heal. The simplest is the best.

Faith, the Essential Ingredient

Jesus was the finest healer the world has ever seen. His healing was done on pure faith.

Did God anoint him with the Holy Spirit and some mystical power? Jesus always stated that God (Father) was with him, that the son can do nothing of himself, but what he seeth the Father doeth. "The Father abiding in me doeth his works. I and the Father are one." By virtue of his union with the source of life and power, he raised the dead and healed all manner of disease.

To me, faith is the one essential for healing.

Healing is giving: it's being of service. I think it should be called love. Love is the greatest healer of all. Compassion is also very important.

Everyone Can Be a Healer

I think that everyone has the potential of becoming a healer, to a lesser or higher degree, and it is really just a matter of degree. Healing is an expression of love in action.

I do not run around and shout, "I'm a healer." If an individual comes to me and asks for help, it is given. I do not go out and look for people to heal.

If people do not want this healing, or don't believe in it, I cannot force it on them. They must want it! There are many who come for healing, when the medical doctors tell them there's nothing more that they can do. As a last resort, they come to a healer. Even then they wait too long.

Miracles do happen, whether it's a mental awakening or a physical healing, or both. I have total faith that God's healing energy flows through me, into my hands and into the body of the patient. I never doubt this for one instant.

Healing Triggers an Energy Flow

I can feel the energy flow even before I place my hands on the patient. The *intent* of healing triggers the energy flow. The intent is that I want this patient healed of all his or her problems. The intent is to become attuned to the patient's spirit, my spirit and to the God spirit. It is all the same spirit.

Each day I affirm to God my thanks for being allowed to be a channel of His healing energy and love. You might say that I am in constant attunement. It's been said that I have spirit guides who assist me in my work, and for that I am thankful.

To acknowledge the guides from time to time is rewarding. For it's when you give up the need to find out who the guides are that they let you know they are there.

Some patients respond much faster than others. There are sometimes instant remissions which are considered miracles. But most of the time, it takes three to four sessions to bring about a normal state of health.

Finding the Cause; Treating the Effect

Much depends upon the condition of the patient's mental outlook. We must get to the cause of the illness and then treat the effect. Many healers just work on the effect. Some have very good results! Yet maybe weeks later, patients return with the same problems. They went back to the same negative environments, and infected themselves with the same emotional problems which manifested into the same ailments they came to the healers to cure.

Many cases are treated in this way. The healer just heals the effect. The patients are so overjoyed and their faith strengthened by the fact that they are free of pain, that faith is the holding affect. There are many who are so negative even after healing, they simply cannot believe it, and the old symptoms return.

I think that every good healer works in a similar way. There are many people calling themselves healers who should be locked up. They make a complete mockery of healing, and this can be very dangerous.

Ego must be stripped away. Of course, there are many healers who do not bring God into it, and yet they are successful. Personally, I don't care how another healer operates, so long as the patient gets better and becomes whole again.

Finding the Trigger Mechanism

If I were to describe my technique, I would say that after patients arrive, I make them comfortable. I get them to open up and talk to me. I find out what their problems are and how long they have had them. I also want to know what their doctors have said about their cases. Then, I start asking questions about their lives.

This reveals quite a bit of useful information and helps me to find the causes of their physical or mental manifestations. Many healers today don't bother trying to find the cause of an illness, they just work on the effect. My healing differs somewhat, in that I probe deeply into patients' psyches to find the *trigger mechanisms* which create the blockages. Once I find a patient's trigger mechanism, the patient validates it, and in many cases, it helps with the final healing.

We Are One In Spirit

After I finish talking with the patient, I close my eyes and make what I call a three-fold attunement; tuning into the patient's spirit, to my spirit, and to God's spirit. For, after all, we are all one spirit.

I stand behind the patient with my hands gently placed upon the patient's head. I begin each healing with a prayer. I pray to God and give thanks that I am able to give healing, that I am a channel for God.

I then feel a surge of energy flowing through my body. My body seems to tingle while my hands begin to vibrate. I allow my hands to be guided to the afflicted areas of the patient's body that are in need of healing.

If I don't feel that inspirational guidance, I do a body balancing, which consists of laying on of hands at the energy centers of the body (chakras).

There is always a good effect after the body balancing. Patients usually respond by saying how peaceful and relaxed they feel. I ask for divine intervention with all my healing. As I stated before, I do nothing. I am just a channel. I listen to the higher wisdom which seems to guide me. I never question. Sometimes I ask if the person can be healed. The answer is always "yes," to whatever level on which I might be working.

5

Pray Yourself Well

One of the most amazing examples of "absent healing," that is, healing a patient who is not in the presence of the healer, occurred with the participation of Agnes Sanford, the wife of an Episcopalian minister from Westboro, Massachusetts. Mrs. Sanford is also the author of an enlightening book on healing entitled *The Healing Light*.

The patient was the eight-year-old daughter of a doctor in Asheville, North Carolina. She had been hospitalized with a virus inflammation of the brain and spinal cord. The child was paralyzed from the neck down, and a 106 degree temperature raged through her tiny body. The young girl was also afflicted by continual convulsions and despite prolonged sedation, doctors were unable to control the spasms.

"Death seemed only a few hours away until the hospital chaplain telephoned Mrs. Sanford," an Asheville doctor related.

Mrs. Sanford asked for one of Asheville's most respected physicians, a personal friend, to place his hands on the child at precisely 9:30 P.M. "I'll begin my prayers at that moment," Mrs. Sanford said.

A witness to the incredible cure through prayer later told the story in his own words:

"The doctor entered the room where a nurse was using chloroform to try to anesthetize the patient so that further convulsions might be prevented. At that time, convulsions were occurring every three or four minutes.

"The doctor placed his hands on the child at precisely 9:30. He had no sooner touched the patient than a relaxed sigh rose from her lips and she fell into a deep, natural sleep. The convulsions ceased and the child seemed very relaxed.

"The following morning, the girl was still sleeping. Her right side was no longer paralyzed and, by afternoon, life came back into her entire body. Ten days later, the patient was released from the hospital and returned to her home."

By the following Christmas, the child was completely cured and the grateful family enjoyed a blessed holiday. The girl grew into a vital, healthy young woman who is the joy of her parents.

"We need not perplex ourselves as to the precise mode in which prayer is answered. It is enough for us to know and feel that it is the most natural, the most powerful, and the most elevated expression of our thoughts and wishes in all great emergencies." *A. P. Stanley*

Praying Creatively

Dr. William A. Tiller tells us that all of the things that we do in life are individual acts of creation. If we are to be effective creators—and learn to pray creatively—there are four important steps he suggests we follow:

1. We must clearly visualize our intention.
2. We must build a strong desire to achieve that intention.
3. We must develop the faith that the visualization can be achieved.
4. We must exercise the will to make it manifest. That is, we must truly work at it.

Struggle and strife, pain and illness are to be anticipated on the Earth plane, Dr. Tiller states: "If the medium in which we wish to create offers us no resistance, then we can make no durable impression. We must expect to struggle!"

The Skepticism of Medical Doctors

Most medical doctors and their colleagues, the psychiatrists, are highly skeptical of any form of faith healing. In a statement on the subject, the American Medical Association denounced the practice by stating: "The medical profession recognizes the power of faith on the individual mind as a factor that may affect the condition of sick people. There are occasional instances in which diseases generally regarded as uniformly fatal reverse themselves without any explainable medical cause, whether or not the patient has had the ministrations of so-called healers.

"If such a phenomenon were to occur to an individual under 'treatment' by one of these healers, the likelihood is that he or she would take the credit. But the medical profession does not recognize that 'faith healing' as such has any accepted merit whereby it can be regarded as having remedial or curative effect in persons who are actually victims of organic disease."

In reference to the A.M.A.'s statement, a noted faith healer commented: "Let us assume a patient is being treated by a licensed medical doctor and the uniformly fatal disease reverses itself. Would not the medical profession assume credit for the cure?"

The Growing Popularity of Faith Healing

Despite its detractors, faith healing has surged forward in the past decades. Newspapers, radio stations and television networks have publicized spiritual healing. Seminarians have investigated the field and written doctoral theses on faith healing. Many ministers are actively seeking more information on the methods and ministrations of faith healing.

In England, Dr. Christopher Woodard believes the power of spiritual healing is as effective as the tools and pills he carries in his black satchel. Writing in *A Doctor Heals by Faith,* this British physician states: "...the next great step forward...is the realization of the existence of healing powers on the spiritual level which, as yet, have not been understood, though they were seen very clearly when Christ was on earth."

Saviour Means Healer

In *The New Healing*, Dr. Paul Tillich of Harvard University's School of Divinity disapproved of the long neglect of Christ-centered spiritual healing by the world's religious leaders. "The gospels, certainly, are not responsible for this disappearance of the power in the picture of Jesus," wrote Dr. Tillich. "They abound in stories of healing; but *we* are responsible ministers, laymen, theologians, who forget that 'Saviour' means 'healer,' he who makes whole and sane what is broken and insane, in body and mind."

Suggestibility plays an important role in faith healing, and no honest healer will deny this influence. Swiss psychologist Heinrich Meng believes there are certain factors which increase the suggestibility factor for those who seek a cure at a healing shrine or service.

"Patients come...looking for divine intervention," reported Dr. Meng. "Religious or not, there is the expectancy of a cure, mingled with anxiety. The patient is prepared to give himself over...to a change of climate, scenery, human contacts, the sense of being present...where miraculous cures have been reported."

Dr. Alexis Carrel won the Nordhoff-Jung medal for cancer research and is convinced of the power of prayer. "Prayer is the most powerful form of energy known to man," declared Dr. Carrel, who won the 1912 Nobel Prize in physiology and medicine. Dr. Carrel saw a vicious cancer sore suddenly transformed into a scar and could scarcely believe his eyes. The miracle occurred after honest, devout prayer by the patient.

The controversy about the worth of faith healing will undoubtedly continue to rage for many decades. People with a strong belief in the supernatural have their faith reaffirmed with each report of a miraculous healing.

Those who are convinced of the total validity of modern science are unable to accept any report of spiritual healing. A single faith healing means their orderly world of dogmatic science will be split with chaotic insecurity.

"Faith, like light, should always be simple and unbending; love like warmth, should beam forth on every side and bend to every necessity of our brethren." *Martin Luther*

Affirm It Is So

Irene F. Hughes, the famous Chicago seer, observes that we can experience healing and an inner calm and peace if we prepare for the happening through prayer and study. Offering her advice for a manifestation of answered prayers, Mrs. Hughes stated:

"We must learn that it is not enough to *ask* for something when we pray. We must *affirm* that it is so. Affirmation shows faith, and in faith comes an overwhelming experience of knowing.

"I feel that we are all becoming more aware that God is within us and not in some far distant Heaven, and that we do not have to seek God in strange places, but to find Him where He really is."

An Experiment in Positive Praying

Sir Alister Hardy, the famed marine biologist, Emeritus Professor at Oxford, insisted to me that one truly can test the power of prayer and actually experiment with it to see that it really works.

"However unlikely it may seem to someone from a rationalistic upbringing," he stated, "try the experiment of really imagining that there is some element with which you can make contact beyond your conscious self. Have *that* amount of faith and see."

Sir Alister admitted that his method of bringing positive prayer results is a very old one with a very recognizable origin. The approach, he stated, should be made as if you were a child speaking to a beloved Father, realizing at the same time that "the form of this relationship is almost certainly a psychological one based upon one's own formal filial affection."

Although you know the reality must be something very different, Sir Alister explains, the visualization enables you to have the emotional sense of devotion that is a necessary part of the process. "The analogy, if you like, sets up the relationship with this element beyond the conscious self."

Once the proper relationship has been established, Sir Alister sets forth the following experiment to "test" the efficacy of prayer:

Ask in all humility to receive help in trying to bring about a better state of the world ("Thy Kingdom come, thy will be done") and think in what ways you might do something to further such a goal.

Ask to be shown how you can keep yourself in better health to play a better and more active part in the world. Ask yourself if you are abusing your own body by taking more than your proper share of daily bread.

Ask that you may realize your own faults and how to mend them, and how to forgive those who have trespassed against you.

Ask that you may recognize with thought what are the real temptations and evils that are making your life less worthy than it could be.

Sir Alister fully believes that if you carry out this experiment with deep feeling and devotion and not simply rattle the prayer through in a matter of seconds, you will come to feel a new power within yourself and feel in touch with a power and a glory beyond yourself "which can make the world a different place, a new kingdom."

Sir Alister also feels that such a prayer as the kind outlined above is as essential to mental health as is physical exercise is to the body: "It clears and uplifts the mind and gives us a zest!"

6

Building a Closer Communion with God

Dr. Harmon Hartzell Bro, author of books on the life readings of Edgar Cayce, the sleeping prophet, offers four simultaneous fronts for building a closer communion with God:

1. Act on your chosen ideals. (Dr. Bro comments that almost all mental illness is caused by individuals attempting to live up to other people's expectations or ideals.)
2. Learn to risk your love in relationships with other people. ("This means risking love and trust and forgiveness even when dealing with minorities, outcasts and strangers," Dr. Bro said.)
3. Study your own experiences of growth. (What are you like when people love to see you arrive and hate to see you go?)
4. Enter into daily meditation. ("In Cayce's terms, meditation was a serious daily cultivation of attuning yourself to God, where the individual will and reason were subordinated to wake up something else.")

"To a certain extent, God gives to the prayerful control of Himself, and becomes their willing agent; and when the time comes when all mysteries are solved, and the record of all lives is truthfully revealed, it will probably be seen that not those who astonished the world with their own powers, but those who quietly, through prayer, used God's power, were the ones who made the world move forward." *E. P. Roe*

The Quiet Healers

Most people consider a faith healer to be a flamboyant spellbinder with hypnotic powers, a conman's lack of conscience and a spiel primed for the collection plate. While there may be healing hucksters in the land, a report by the National Council of Churches on faith healing in American Protestantism indicates that many reputable ordained ministers regularly practice some form of faith healing.

The report was prepared by Dr. Charles A Branden, a professor of Religion and Literature of Religions at Northwestern University. More than 30 percent of the ministers who replied to his questionnaire reported that they had healed sixty-four different diseases through prayer.

"The Branden Report was only a survey. There was no obligation for ministers to submit detailed medical reports," said an officer of the National Council of Churches. "Nevertheless, the respondents were very conservative in their claims."

Dr. Branden pointed out this same conclusion in the report. "In almost every case, the informant declared that the diagnosis had been made by a competent medical doctor. There had been medical treatment for a period of time," said Dr. Branden. "One case of cancer of the lungs had persisted for two years and was properly diagnosed and treated by a physician. After the healing, which consisted of laying on of the hands, some ritual and prayer at a healing service, X-ray tests disclosed the condition had cleared. In a period of six months prior to the reporting of the case there had been no recurrence."

The Healing Power of Prayer

Another minister, from the Midwest, told of curing a thirty-seven-year-old woman of lung cancer. Only a week prior to the healing, she had been examined by several consulting physicians and told that she had only a few days to live. The minister prayed with the woman. She confessed her sins. She also forgave a woman whom she hated. Her lungs were clear of cancer on the following morning and, after several years, the woman remains cured of the dread affliction.

A Colorado pastor prayed with a Denver man who had been bedfast for almost two years. Physicians had unsuccessfully treated the patient's tubercular condition and, finally, had abandoned all hope of recovery for the man. Following prayer and laying on of the hands, a cure was immediately effected.

"The condition disappeared. The man was back at work within two days," reported the minister. There is no disease that cannot be cured by prayer!

Eighty percent of the healing ministers reported their cures were "permanent." In many instances, several years had passed since the healing had occurred; there was no evidence of recurrence of the disease. Dr. Branden, like many others, considered any healing which lasted for two years to be "permanent."

Apparently there is absolutely no disease that cannot be healed by prayer. The ministers who have this gift of healing claim a lack of miraculous power in their hands. "There isn't any magic or strange power to it," declared an Episcopalian minister who regularly holds healing services. "It is not the minister's hands, but God who does the healing!"

"The first petition that we are to make to Almighty God is for a good conscience, the next for health of mind, then of body." *Seneca*

Advice from a Master Sensitive

The much respected sensitive Harold Sherman provided this tip for anyone seeking to develop the inner powers that humankind possesses:

"If you try too hard, you activate your imagination and then you self-hallucinate. That is a very important point. It isn't a case of being deserving, as we would try to determine our meriting a revelation, a healing, a burst of psychic ability. "We achieve such experiences when our own mental attitudes or emotional natures happen to be right.

"We hit a higher frequency for a moment—and all of a sudden something happens."

Prayerfully Entering the Holy Silence

Dream-teachings and visions of guidance and healing may be obtained by sincere and respectful journeys into the silence of meditation and altered states of consciousness.

In the Holy Silence is the most sacred of energies concentrated. When you enter the Great Silence, you will feel and know that it is composed of the vibrations of Cosmic Light. You will sense around you the presence of great master teachers and highly evolved intelligences.

The essence of the Silence is the power of the Light and unconditional love. And pulsating deep within such light and such love is the essence of the Source of All-That-Is.

Prior to seeking a vision, a healing, a profound inspiration, sit quietly.

Summon the Silence to you. Feel the essence of it focused in your spiritual center (visualized for mental assistance as your crown chakra) and in your physical center (visualized for mental assistance as your heart chakra). Know that the Divine Energy of the Silence has permeated the spiritual and physical pivots of your own essence.

Be still within and without, knowing that the Source has entered all levels of your consciousness and all levels of your being. Know that you now have the ability to focus this holy energy on the part of your body—or the body of another—that needs healing.

Although we realize intellectually that the Source is an energy, it does aid us in achieving the transfer if we visualize it as an individualized presence.

Some still prefer the image of a loving Father or Mother. Others focus upon the image of a glowing Light Being.

Since we humans seem to communicate more effectively with images that most resemble us, I always encourage people to develop a personal idea of a loving intelligence that is ready to answer their every call, that is willing to grant every request that is for their good, their gaining, and their healing of body and mind.

It is truly important that you visualize and attempt to feel the reality of that individualized presence above you. Know that it is connected to you by a ray of light, a stream of energy that flows into your body through your crown chakra.

If you like, you may verbalize your love of the Source and call the name of a holy figure or master teacher to aid you in intensifying the transmission. Many people have said that they have actually felt a warmth touching their crown chakra while sending love to the Source.

Just remember that the summoning of a vision or a request for healing must always be the result of a balanced desire.

Take three comfortably deep breaths, holding each for the count of three. Feel At-One with the essence of the Source that has blended with you.

Visualize a golden flame within your heart chakra. In your consciousness, travel a ray of golden light from your heart to the Source of All-That-Is that still exists above you. Understand that, powerful and beautiful as the feeling of the Source is within you, your soul energy can absorb only an infinitesimal percentage of its true majesty. You must now send a beam of your essence to the Source that vibrates in a dimension above you.

Feel yourself coming closer to the Source of All-That-Is.

See points of violet light touching every cell of your physical body as your light body begins to connect with your Higher Self. Begin to sense strongly a closeness, an at-one-ment with the Source. Begin to feel healing energy entering your body.

Concentrate for a moment on making your body as still as possible. Direct your attention to the Source and focus on the flame within your heart chakra. See clearly the ray of light that you are transmitting to the Source of All-That-Is.

Now feel your consciousness melding with Higher Consciousness and begin to request a vision or a healing manifestation.

Eliminate awareness of the physical body as much as it is possible for you to do so. Understand your body as a connection to the Earth and nothing more. Visualize it pure, unblemished, holy—and completely healed!

Visualize yourself holding open hands to the Source, as if you were about to receive some object of a material substance from It.

Mentally affirm the following:

"Source of All-That-Is, give me strength, energy, and courage. Grant that I receive all that I need for my good, my gaining, and my total wellness."

Visualize the Source as the eternally powerful energy that ignites the golden flame that burns within your own heart chakra. The more profoundly that you can visualize this connection, the greater the results of your healing.

7

Change Your Fear into Faith

Dorothy Spence Lauer taught that there are three steps in visualization:

1. Selection
2. Visualization
3. Gratitude

If you have previously tried visualization without success, you may have omitted one of the above steps. Visualization cannot become reality until all the steps have been fulfilled. You must have completeness of procedure in order to bring into actualization your mental images of health.

However, Mrs. Lauer also warned that if you hold in your mind a vivid image of something you fear, such as being stricken with a disease, your fear sometimes can cause the disease to manifest within the physical body.

"Why not change your fear into faith, knowing that you can just as well be healthy and happy instead of being miserable and unhappy?" she would ask. "Our minds must be trained to be ready to put aside fear and disbelief."

After a visualization for health, happiness, etc., has materialized, it is time to take the third step.

"I often say to people, 'You now have acquired what it was you selected and visualized. Haven't you forgotten something?'

"They usually answer, 'I can't imagine what I've forgotten.'

"At this point, they are in for a session with me on the importance of being grateful. Often I will say to them: 'When you wanted health, you devoted many hours to hoping, selecting, and thinking how wonderful it would be, yet it only takes a second to be grateful!'

"'Father, I thank Thee that Thou hast heard me, and I know Thou hearest me always,' is a favorite prayer of gratitude that I use.

"But I often reverse the procedure and give thanks before I receive what I want!"

Keep Your Faith Strong

In the words of Dorothy Spence Lauer:

I always warn everyone, be certain that what you visualize is really what you want, for you will surely receive it!

You must desire and act as if the health condition you wish were actually now present. And, as I have stressed, you must give thanks for the realization of your desires before the deed has truly been accomplished.

You can affirm and daydream all day and achieve no results. I have letters in my files saying, "I affirmed that my health would be better and it's worse." I have then attempted to show these people where they were in error: they did not act as if they were better!

If a person were to say, "I'm better," but not wholeheartedly believe it, or desire it hard enough, or visualize how he would feel if he were no longer ill, and if he were afraid to give thanks for something which, as yet, he had not received, his condition would not improve.

My faith has been strong since I was a child. In Sunday School the teacher would say, "How many of you have had your prayers answered?" Invariably, my hand would go up.

The Bible says, "Ask, believing you shall receive, and you

shall." To this day I still am answering my Sunday School teacher's question. I cannot understand anyone *not* having sufficient faith in God to truly believe.

Healing "Congealed Life"

No doubt you have heard of many miraculous healings. Healing is really a loosening of congestion. Congestion is congealed life. When the congestion is gone, out flows miraculous healing.

Through emotion, you can liquefy that which you wish healed. Fervent emotion (strong, but not hysterical or wild) will cause the liquefying process to take place, and your strong conviction will produce the results of healing.

Churches provide beautiful music to arouse the emotions. The leaders of churches are often intelligent, learned individuals, who know that the emotional fire that burns within releases the condition that causes illness. Here is the secret of miraculous healing. By "emotion" I do not mean to imply wild or hysterical excitement; I mean only a conviction of healing so deep that it hastens the curative processes.

I do not think that anyone should take credit for healing another person, because, truly, Universal Mind does the healing *through* the person who has the conviction that he or she is healed. It is the natural law that accomplishes healings.

The Laws of the Mind Are Universal

When you are grieving over something, have you noticed that nothing tastes good? And that no matter how you exercise, you seem to be devitalized? I was acquainted with someone who always felt ill when faced with responsibility. When she was relieved of the responsibility, she would feel positively wonderful again.

Have you ever heard the story about the man who was always very healthy? One day his friends decided to try to upset him, each one saying to him, "My, you look bad today.

Don't you feel well?" By the end of the day he was a very sick man. The thoughts of poor health became so deeply imbedded in his mind that he actually became quite ill.

When my children first entered school, I checked the long list of children's diseases on their health cards and wrote the word "No" on the back of each one of them. The doctor was quite surprised. I told him that the only thing they had ever had was a very slight case of measles.

Their records remain the same today...not one disease has been marked. We have never talked illness, felt illness, or been unduly concerned when around ill people. I do not mean to imply that we do not need medical doctors. On the contrary, I have the utmost admiration and respect for them. By all means, consult your doctor if you are ill. My point is that many people think themselves sick by worrying about "catching" a disease or because they expect to become ill.

Have you ever noticed when a new disease is discovered and its symptoms appear in the newspapers that very soon you hear of more people reporting the same symptoms? The thought of the disease became so strong in their minds that the attraction took place. They actually attracted the disease to them.

The Power of Words

Words are most powerful. Let us say that you visualize the things you want, yet your words are different from what you visualize. If you have visualized that you are healthy and happy, but continue to tell your friends that you do not feel well, that you are utterly disgusted with life in general, and so on, you are counteracting the visualized picture with conflicting words. Therefore, conditions may go from bad to worse, because although the visualization is powerful, your words are also a potent force.

The word is as powerful as thought. Combine the right word with visualization and you have the perfect combination to bring your goals and desires into your life.

Words and Thoughts: A Potent Mixture

You must come to the conclusion that your spoken words and your thoughts are the most important things that you can exercise in the right way.

A former acquaintance of mine had a very tasteless sense of humor. She was the type of a person who would call you on the phone and say that she had gone to the doctor and was told she had cancer. Unless you knew this person, you would naturally feel shocked and sorry for her. Then a few days later, she would call up and tell you that she had been joking!

Now I wonder if you can guess what happened to this particular person? You see, she had been putting that powerful word into effect. She had said she had cancer so many times to so many people, that she had placed this powerful thought not only in her own subconscious, but in the thoughts of her friends.

The day came when she did have cancer. You can imagine the shock that was in her voice the day she called and said, "I'm really not joking, I do have cancer!"

I tried to be very understanding with her, but also reminded her that I had warned her so many times that the day would come when she would be like the boy who cried "Wolf!" No one answered when the wolf really was there.

This woman never got over the shock of her condition, but it did teach her a lesson. She was very careful from that day forward. She had learned that part of the lesson, but I am sorry to say, it was just a little too late. However, she later went out of her way many times to help other people see the error of their ways.

Visualize A God of Love

When confronted with a serious problem, I again say that you should always remember to make God the first to be honored.

If you are troubled, ill or wondering about the outcome of anything, I suggest that you say: "The Spirit of the Lord goes before me and makes easy and successful my way."

Do not doubt! Here again is the law in action—you are saying the way will be easy for you.

It is only for you to take command of your life and shape it accordingly. Anyone who says, "It is the will of God that I'm ill," is very wrong. Yet many people believe this, so they continue on their way, believing their misery is God's will. That I shall never believe!

I am going to say something here that I hope you will accept and understand: sometimes people are just too lazy to exert themselves, so making the "will of God" responsible makes it easy for them to drift along, getting nowhere.

If we are to believe the Bible, how can we not also believe that, "As your faith is, so shall it be to you."

God will be to you just as you imagine Him to be. If you decide He is a stern judge, dealing out misfortune and misery, then that is what He will be to you. Change your concept of God to that of a deity who gives you abundant health, happiness, love, and see what a different God He appears to be.

Wish Thy Neighbor Well

You should also realize that consideration of your neighbor is very important. Remember the commandment to love your neighbor as yourself? This does not mean that you have to love as a friend a neighbor whom you do not particularly care for, but you should hold a certain degree of deep inner conviction that you wish that person well.

You cannot expect to visualize all good things for yourself and never once think of your neighbor. It only takes a second to send a blessing to the person who may be tired, who may be sorrowful; and you do not even have to tell that person you are doing this. You will, however, notice added changed in your neighbor's life that will make you smile secretly to yourself, because you have used this powerful law for the other person's benefit, wishing him or her well.

When your own dear ones say something to hurt your feelings, instead of being angry with them, sit down quietly and send them a silent message, a blessing. This will work much faster than a telephone call or a telegram, because these thoughts reach others so quickly that harmony will take over. But if you harbor negative thoughts toward others, you will find that they cause you to be ill, unpleasantly depressed, and irritable.

Be Cautious of the Law of Retribution

You must *never* visualize anyone becoming ill or passing away. This is something that I am very much against, and I always caution against it. It is not right.

If you ever attempt it, remember it *can* work, but the law of retribution will have to be paid back by you—perhaps by suffering the very thing that you caused that other person to go through.

We are not put here to hurt other people, nor to judge them. We all have enough to take care of our own lives.

Be Cautious When Praying for Another

Just as we should remember Phillips Brooks' observation that in its simplest definition, "A prayer is merely a wish turned God-ward," so we must remind ourselves that worry is nothing more than negative prayer. It is much better to "let go and let God," than to stress ourselves with worries that only increase our nervousness, self-consciousness, and our ill health.

As Socrates demonstrated long ago, our prayers should be for blessings in general, for God surely knows best what is good for us.

We must also be very cautious in praying for the healing

of another. Strange as it may seem to us, our loved one's illness may be soul-chosen for that person's good and gaining. Suffering and pain often serve as the crucible in which the soul is purified and cleansed. More than one wise observer of our species' spiritual evolution has pointed out that very often God's way of answering a prayer for patience and love is to place that person in a furnace of affliction.

Tyron Edwards said it well when he wrote: "The end of our prayers is often gained by an answer very different from what we expect. 'Lord, what wilt Thou have me to do?' was the question of Paul; and a large part of the answer was, 'I will show him what great things he must suffer.'"

As William Penn put it: "No pain, no palm; no thorns, no throne; no gall, no glory; no cross, no crown."

8

Huna Healing Prayers

In February of 1972, I visited the Hawaiian Islands and had an opportunity to study Huna healing techniques at first hand. For some time prior to my trip I had been professionally associated with Max Freedom Long, who in 1917 had become intrigued by the tales of the Kahunas, the "keepers of the secret." Long spent several years in Hawaii in an attempt to crack the secret code of the Kahunas; and by the time of his death on September 23, 1971, he was considered by many to be the world's greatest authority on the Polynesian psycho-religious system known as Huna.

As a young schoolteacher in Hawaii, Max Freedom Long at first could find no native islander who would speak to him at any length about Huna. Long kept at his research, for he was undergoing a personal spiritual search, and the native religion seemed to offer yet another avenue of psychic exploration.

At last Max met Dr. William Tufts Brigham, curator of the Bishop Museum, a man heavy with both scientific honors and girth. Dr. Brigham took a liking to the earnest young seeker, and told the enthralled young schoolteacher how the Kahunas accomplished astounding healings and amazing feats of psychic phenomena.

"They have a system of psychology and religion which is pure enough and close enough to its source—whatever that may have been—to work for them," Dr. Brigham said.

"If you want to study it and try to learn the secret behind what they did, remember to watch for three things: some unit of *consciousness* guiding some *unit* of force making it work through some f*orm of substance.* I know that the secret will be very scientific when you find it, but it has eluded me for forty years!"

Many years later, Max Freedom Long returned to the mainland in defeat. His conscious mind had exhausted every avenue of research, but his unconscious mind had not yet raised the white flag of surrender.

He was awakened one night in 1935 by a bursting light energy which seemed to suffuse the entire room and which shook his intellect with the frenzy of sudden revelation.

He no longer saw through a glass darkly.

It occurred to him with his new insight that since the Kahunas had names for elements in their magic, these words might be found in the Hawaiian-English dictionary that had begun to be formulated as early as 1820. He knew that the Hawaiian language is constructed from short root words and that a translation of the root usually gives the original meaning of a word.

He sat down with his immense volume of personal notes and began to sort the accumulated research of over forty years' study that had been bequeathed to him by Dr. Brigham.

It was this revelation that enabled Max Freedom Long to crack the ancient code of the Kahunas.

The Essence of Huna

The very essence of Huna lies in the belief that we possess three souls: the *uhane*, a weak, animal-like spirit that talks; the *unihipili*, a secretive spirit that sticks to, and often hides, another spirit; and the *Aumakua*, the older parental spirit, composed of both male and female elements, that has the low self (unihipili) and the middle self (uhane) under its guidance.

In psychological terms, one might say that, centuries before Freud, the Kahunas had discovered the conscious (uhane), the unconscious (unihipili), and the superconscious (Aumakua).

"I had found the three elements which Dr. Brigham had stipulated any successful system of magic must employ," Max said. "I determined that Huna works as a system because it contains a *form of consciousness* that directs the magical processes, a *force* utilized by the consciousness that provides the necessary power, and a *substance*, visible or invisible, through which the force can act."

The Aumakua, or High Self, is the "god" within each person. It is on this level above our waking, conscious level, that we have the power to perform miracles.

"The one rule of life in Huna is that no man should do anything that might hurt another," Max often stated.

"The only sin is to harm another human being,"

The more advanced Kahunas added loving service to their fellow beings to this rule.

Our Three Bodies

According to Huna belief, each individual's three spirits are surrounded, or encased, in three shadowy bodies composed of a substance called *aka*. Each of our bodies is fed by its own supply of *mana*, the vital force.

The low self (unihipili) utilizes simple mana; the middle self (uhane) feeds on a more highly charged mana-mana; the High Self (Aumakua) operates on mana-loa.

It is the role of the middle self to instruct the low self to store an extra supply of mana. This store of mana is to be held in readiness for the time when it is necessary to reach up the connecting aka cord and make contact with the High Self.

It is the High Self, the "god" within, that brings about the desired conditions asked in those prayers formed by the combined efforts of the three selves.

The Aka Cord

Max believed that he had found strong evidence that the Egyptians were equally aware of the aka threads.

"In some of the drawings in the tombs we see a spider pictured hanging by a thread of web above a mummy case," he explained. "The spider was the symbol of the aka, or shadowy thread, at its best. In the outer teachings, it was said that one had to climb a thread of spider web to get up to heaven.

"The cord that goes between the body and the High Self is made up of many threads, forming a cord—the silver cord mentioned in the Old Testament.

"In Huna, the web with the spider in the center, with threads reaching out in all directions, was the favorite symbol used to describe the mechanism.

"In Tibet there was once a whole system of belief developed in which the universe was said to be like a web and the souls of humans like tiny spiders dotted here and there over the vast web.

"The aborigines in Australia still have a sacred string which is a part of their magic kit.

"On Easter Island, the umbilical cord was the symbol, and such cords were carefully preserved after birth.

"In Polynesia, the word for low self (unihipili) had several meanings, one of which was 'sticky.' This refers to the aka threads which, like the thread of web exuded by a spider, is at first sticky and will adhere to anything."

Max Freedom Long believed that the "silver cord" of aka substance is our means of contact with our High Selves. It is the "telephone line" we use when we call up to ask for help or just to say that we love life.

This "telephone wire" has mana as its electricity, mana which flows from the low to the High Self, then back again when we use the mystic phone in prayer or worship.

Telepathy, Max Long maintained, is the conversation of two or more people along the telephone wire of aka substance. It employs the same mechanism as conversation with the High Self.

And it is most important to realize that *all prayer is telepathic,* and all telepathy is made up of messages sent in picture form by the low self.

How to Send Pictures to Your High Self

Max gave careful advice as to how best to send the proper pictures to the High Self:

If you picture yourself in perfect health and impress that image on the low self as the thing to send as a "want" to your High Self, the low self will create a picture of you in perfect health and will send the picture.

The way the High Self answers the prayer is "make real" or "materialize" the picture into reality for you. This is the secret of secrets in Huna.

But, the picture of perfect health must *not* be one that includes your sickness.

If you pray, "Heal my illness," the low self will make a picture of you sick and miserable and send it for the prayer. With it will go a picture of you wanting something and perhaps an image of you as well and healthy. The result is a muddle and nothing is given to the High Self to change your condition.

You must believe that you are receiving perfect health already.

You must hold the thought of yourself as well and happy. If you do not, you inevitably send a sick picture to the High Self to spoil the good picture of perfect health that you have already sent up in prayer.

Making the picture of perfect health must be done with the use of the mana in order to get a lasting memory or thought-form picture to keep recalling and sending frequently to the High Self.

Make and memorize your picture with breathing in order to collect the mana and give the picture enough strength to hold together while the High Self materializes it into actuality for you.

Instruct your low self to send the picture and plenty of

mana to the High Self, like a telepathic message. The low self already knows how, so just set it to work.

Repeat your prayer action at least once a day and continue until the answer is given.

Have faith.

Tell yourself that perfect health is already given on the level of the High Self and is already real.

Live in the picture.

Feel it.

Keep your mind off your ills.

Your Blueprint to Health

Max always cautioned the neophyte healer that the first step in administering the curative touch is to breathe deeply, slowly, rhythmically. At the same time, silently ask your low self to manufacture a large mana charge.

When you feel that you are well "charged up," make a mental picture of yourself and your low self causing the patient to be in perfect health. When this is accomplished, picture the call being made to your High Self.

"Don't *talk* the picture, as that just makes words, and the low and High Selves need pictures constructed of mana-strengthened thought-forms," Max emphasized.

"Keep your mouth shut and your mind open! The mental picture is your plan, your blueprint, your road map...the mold which will be used to remold the conditions of illness to perfect health."

Once you have the picture firmly in mind, advance to your patient and place your fingers lightly on the place that hurts or that is injured and requires healing.

If, for one reason or another, it is impossible to touch the injured area, touch the subject's hand or head, then hold your hands a small distance away from the subject's body on either side of the troubled area.

"The low self can project the mana through the shadowy thread the touch establishes if you mentally request it to do so," Max said.

"While holding your hands in position, retain the picture in your mind of the call going to your High Self, then of the mana flowing through your fingers and into your patient to charge up the part to be restored."

According to Kahuna methodology, the treatment can last a minute or two, then the healer can pull away, recharge with mana. Repeat the treatment as many times as you feel is necessary.

You should always end by giving silent thanks to the High Self and then to the low self. Then wash your hands while telling yourself that you are washing all the subject's illness or imperfections down the drain, never to return. Such a "down the drain" procedure will keep you from possibly picking up your patient's pains through suggestion.

Once when Max Long was asked if the Huna healing methods were not, in essence, the very ancient practice of "laying on of hands," he replied that it most certainly is.

"But in Huna we learn what, besides making a prayer, we are to do in the ancient healing ritual," he explained.

"One does not have to touch the person who is being treated after an aka thread of contact has been established. So-called 'absent healing' makes good use of the aka threads without knowing that they are doing so. Look at a person, hear his voice or see his picture, and your low self can pick up a thread and follow it in a flash in order to contact the person."

Prayer: The Central Theme of Huna

Max Freedom Long believed the central theme of Huna to be prayer and the obtaining of answers to prayer. He learned that when the Kahunas were still at work in old Hawaii they had a ritual in which the native priest withdrew from the sight of the people gathered before the crude temple platform and entered a grass house reserved for "braiding the cord." Out of sight, perhaps with a chant, he gathered the aka threads from the silent worshippers, who were praying for the good of the land, and braided, or united, them into a single strong strand which would reach to the High Selves who were watching.

The Kahuna made a mental picture of the land as it should be and sent this image as the "seed" of the prayer to the High Selves so they could grow into reality. His prayer was not a brief one. It was a lengthy ritual done under various taboos. If the prayer was performed correctly, results were expected in due course of time.

Prayer Seeds

In the Huna code, the word for "braid" was *u-la-na.* The first root, *u* is "I, myself," the same as the one used in *u-hane* for the middle self. It tells us that *we* are to do the work of praying.

The root *la* is "light," the symbol for the High Self, telling us to whom the prayer is to be sent.

The combined roots (*lana*) mean "to float," which symbolizes the flow of mana along the braided cord. The steam of mana carries with it the thought forms of the prayer, the "seeds" of the prayer.

In Hawaiian, the word for "worship" is *ho-ana. Ho* is from the root "to make." *Ano* is a seed.

In the Huna code we learn that the act of worship is to create a prayer "seed" to send with the accumulated mana along the aka cord to the High Self.

The Hawaiian word for the answer to a prayer is *ano-hou.* Once again we find the root for "seed" and the root *hou*, which has several meanings. *Hou* may be translated "to make new or to restore," or "to change a form or appearance."

"*Hou* also means 'to pant or to breathe heavily,'" Max said.

Deeper breathing is necessary to accumulate the mana which will carry the seed along the aka cord to the High Self. The mana helps make the High Self strong so it can answer our prayers and make the seed idea grow into reality.

"The united, or blended, male and female selves, who

graduate up from the middle-self level to become a new High Self, are still in a way like the lower selves in the body, and are in need of a form of 'sex union' to start the creative act of making the answer for the prayer...The lore of India has many statues of the gods in close sexual embrace.

"The true meaning of this divine cohabitation seems to be that our prayers and gifts of mana cause the High Selves to come together in a slightly closer union in order to engage in some form of activity which parallels our sex act in that it is the beginning of their creating something."

The Healing Circle

Max Freedom Long learned that some groups who studied Huna sought to project mana through the hands of the members of a healing circle, and to use their combined "wills" to make the mana flow into someone upon whom their hands had been laid. In addition, they might recite a prayer of healing, such as the following:

"Father-Mother, we hold this friend of ours to the Light for healing. Give him/her *life*."

Max advised that one might compose a prayer that would suit all the members of a healing circle, but once the group had decided upon such a prayer, it should be recited only by the leader of the circle, while all other members remained with their hands on the subject in a quiet and prayerful attitude. The prayerful quiet should be held for a least half a minute, then the leader of the circle should end the group prayer with the words of the Kahunas of old.

"Our prayer takes flight. Let the rain of blessings fall. *Ah-mana-mana.*"

"The idea is to close the prayer action and not let it hang dangling," admonished Max.

"Mana goes where it is directed and does what it is asked to do if one has full confidence so that one's low self believes that what is being done will get results.

"Mana will travel or be projected not only by direct physical contact (which is easiest), but along the line of sight to a person.

"The help that one can give oneself with self-suggestion is also great, but like other ways of projecting or manipulating the manas of the body, one must slowly train the low self and get it to understand what part it is to play in the work."

Determined Prayer Commands

Max Freedom Long's careful analysis of Huna convinced him that if a person felt that his or her life might be improved upon in various ways, the application of a simple technique, practiced with determination, could bring about the desired changes.

First, Max advised, you must determine precisely what it is you want, then decide to take steps to obtain it.

Get a small journal or account book that may be carried in your pocket or purse.

"Write down all the things that you want to try to do or become with the help of the low self and the High Self. You will practice self-suggestion on the one, and prayer on the other," Max said.

"Go through the list and pick out the things you feel are most important to you and to those near and dear to you.

"That done, write out the commands you will use in self-suggestion. For instance: 'I am eating the right amounts of the right food every day.'

"When you have worked out and written several commands to your satisfaction, memorize them. Get the High Self to help by accumulating mana and by sending the thought-forms of the prayer-commands to it.

"Get off by yourself. Tense one or two muscles at a time and relax them completely. Recall your commands and use them to order your low self to help: 'I am becoming a better person. I am getting better and better.'

"In the relaxed condition, your low self will accept the suggestions and act on them. *Believe* that you are obeying the commands. That's all there is to it!"

9

Whatsoever You Ask in My Name

by

Sherry Hansen Steiger

Reverend Sherry Hansen Steiger is one of the founding members of the Wholistic Healing Board through the Institute of Health and Education, in Washington, D.C. She also is a licensed massage therapist and has conducted stress management seminars throughout the United States. Rev. Steiger is founder of the Butterfly Center for Transformation and co-creator of the highly acclaimed Celebrate Life Program. She is an ordained minister, a former student and staff member of the Lutheran School of Theology in Chicago, and she has ministered to thousands in settings ranging from community work (the Chicago ghetto, with Martin Luther King and Jesse Jackson in the 1960s) to leadership training programs and crisis counseling. In this chapter she writes of the healing power of prayer.

"Truly, truly I say to you, he who believes in me will also do the works that I do, and greater works than these will he do, because I go to the Father." John 14:6-12

When I was a little girl I would hear the words of Jesus echo through my mind and I would wonder how they might apply to me and my life as well as for all of humankind.

My nursing and seminary studies provided much data to assimilate, but not until I read Gina Cerminara's *Many Mansions* while on internship in 1968-69 did the mystery begin to make sense. I hungered to read other books about Edgar Cayce and related books on healing. My personal frustration with the limitations of medicine and theology now took on expanding possibilities that fit all that I believed in my heart about being a mind, body, and spirit—a total being—not to be separated but to be worked with as a unit—wholistically (a word and concept unheard of at that time). I also had a deep understanding of the continuation of life, of spirit, but my understanding seemed completely alien to the perspectives of my religious upbringing and education.

The Power of a Prayer Group

I took part in an Edgar Cayce 'Search for God' prayer group and began meditating faithfully. There were seeds taking root...the discipline of which began to nourish the fertile soil that would answer my prayers to bring healing to my brothers and sisters for whom I have always had the greatest compassion and desire to help.

Over the years I've had many experiences with the power of prayer, and will share with you several that stand out in my memory.

One evening in 1972, my son Erik was ill with a low fever. I was torn between remaining home with him and attending my regular prayer-healing group meeting. I finally decided that I should attend the meeting and project healing toward Erik, who so desperately needed the prayer energy. I told Paul, my husband, that he should place his hands on Erik at the regularly appointed hour during which the group focused their collective prayer.

As things worked out, our normal healing circle time was

altered by over an hour because of a long discussion, but when we got to it, I sat in for Erik. The group laid hands on me and prayed for his healing.

When I arrived home, Paul, who had been asleep on the couch, sprang up with tremendous excitement to share his story. It seemed that Erik's temperature had shot up to 104 while I was gone. At first Paul had panicked, but then he consoled himself with the thought that God would heal Erik through our prayer circle. He consoled himself so thoroughly that he fell asleep.

When he had awakened, he looked at the clock and saw that he had slept through the time when he was to lay hands on Erik and he felt guilty. Erik, however, who had fallen asleep on the couch with him, got up and began to make his way up the stairs. Startled, Paul demanded that Erik come back and lie down. "It's all right, Daddy," Erik told him. "Mommy's prayer healed me now. I'm all right now. I'm going to get my toys."

Paul took Erik's temperature and was astonished to see that it was normal.

Later, when Paul told me the time that he had awakened and that Erik's fever had broken, it was minutes after the *actual* laying-on-of-hands had taken place.

"The angels may have wider spheres of action and nobler forms of duty than ourselves, but truth and right to them and to us are one and the same thing." *E. H. Chapin*

Another evening, our prayer group received a phone call from the husband of one of the members saying Brenda wasn't able to come. She'd had an accident, and he asked if someone could sit in for her. We weren't told what the accident was, but when I sat in for Brenda in our healing circle, I picked up that her arm was broken. Once again, our time for the healing was not on schedule. I mention this because it seemed more validating for all of us that an actual energy was at work immediately.

What we found out later was truly amazing. Brenda had

broken her arm—a double fracture. She had gone to the hospital and had x-rays, but she refused treatment. She stubbornly insisted that her husband take her home until after our prayer time. She was crying and in much pain at the time we should have been in our circle. Her husband got mad at her and wanted to take her to the doctor, since no healing had taken place.

Then, at exactly the time we sat in for her with laying-on-of-hands, she felt a ring of fire start at her feet and move slowly up her body to her head and down again. When it left, so did her pain. She called us in ecstasy!

She went back to the hospital for a confirmation, and new x-rays showed no break. She said she had fun telling the doctor it was a prayer healing group that had channeled God's healing energy!

Many years later I rushed home after work to pick up my six-year-old daughter Melissa and the babysitter to go to dinner. The babysitter put Melissa on her lap and slammed the door to the car—with Melissa's hand in it.

Melissa's screaming didn't jar the babysitter into having any idea what had happened. She seemed in shock and couldn't respond to me telling her to open the door.

I got out, ran around the car, opened the door, held Melissa's hand in prayer, got back in and raced to the hospital. Her whole hand was crushed.

While we were awaiting the results of the x-rays, Melissa's unceasing screams pierced my heart. I asked the babysitter to join me in prayer. All of a sudden Melissa stopped crying. The doctor came in...Melissa's hand looked nearly normal. The doctor took the x-rays again. The babysitter broke down crying, releasing much tension. She told me that she had never prayed before and wanted me to explain more about God and prayer.

"Whatever you ask in my name, I will do it, that the Father may be glorified in the Son; if you ask anything in my name, I will do it." John 14:13-14

10

The Wonder of Spiritual Healing

Healing is certainly one of the most beautiful acts of sharing that can occur between human beings, and I have always held the utmost respect for those men and women who have devoted their life energies to the healing arts. At the same time, I have often pondered just what healing really is. Is it truly an energy force which can be channeled...or is it largely a matter of faith in the healer's ability to serve as an agent of the God force?

As the result of a series of experiments which he had been conducting since the 1950s, Dr. Bernard Grad, an associate professor in the department of psychiatry at McGill University, Montreal, believes that the laying on of hands channels an actual healing force. In his opinion, the religious rite of laying on of hands releases a force or energy that can be measured under laboratory conditions. In addition, he is convinced that an "unseen energy or force" is released in all forms of human contact, from a kiss to the shaking of hands.

Dr. Grad attests to different qualities of healing energy, and he states: "A personal element of the healer may go along with this power, and if he or she is not moved by true selflessness and concern for others, the results could be negative. The healer must be concerned about his own spiritual state and live a moral life."

Although some of the claims which Cleve Backster, the polygraph expert in *The Secret Life of Plants*, has made regarding plant communication are controversial, his experiments are relevant to a discussion of healing because they imply that all life is one, that there is a signal linkage which exists among all living things, that there is unity to all creation. Such belief is basic to the essential philosophies of all the great metaphysicians of history.

In his book *Blueprint for Immortality*, Dr. Harold Saxton Burr hypothesizes that humans, animals and vegetables have distinctive electrical field patterns. If a universal electrodynamic field exists and flows through every living thing, then science may one day fully accredit the ancient custom of laying on of hands through the instrumentation of its own technology.

Dr. Paul E. Morentz, chief of the psychiatric service of a Veterans Administration Hospital in California, has pointed out that faith healing preceded the medical profession by many centuries.

"Our advances in modern medicine often make us forget that the body has enormous powers to heal itself if these can be brought to bear on the illness," Dr. Morentz said. "It is imperative that we keep an open and inquiring mind about the whole phenomenon of healing."

Sharing the God Force

Al G. Manning is a minister of spiritual science who conducts the ESP laboratory in Los Angeles. Many years ago Manning became seriously interested in the spiritual-metaphysical-faith healing area—the powers which transcend those of the human mind.

"I was suffering from severe migraine headaches, a stomach ulcer problem and the misery of wearing two pair of glasses—one for my close work in accounting and one for distance," says Manning. "Several doctors had used me for a guinea pig with many experiments on the migraine-stomach problems, but to absolutely no avail.

"I maintain my respect for the medical profession," Manning is quick to emphasize, "but I look upon them as *students* of the healing arts and sciences, just as we are. However, I never consider our healing work on a patient complete until his doctor confirms it."

Some years ago, when I met Manning he was healthier than he had ever been. He had no stomach or migraine problems at all, and he had not worn prescription glasses of any kind for about ten years. "At their last testing, my eyes remained 20/20," Manning remarked. "Not the weak things that needed glasses years ago."

The Living Light

Manning cured himself of his afflictions through prayer and the manipulation of energy which he terms the "Living Light."

"This whole thing," Manning states, "has evolved over a number of years of investigating Theosophy, Rosicrucianism, Spiritualism, and 'mystery schools,' but also through what I am impressed to call simply 'spirit guidance.'

"At the time I was ordained a Minister of Spiritual Science, I claimed the healing work as my credential, not this thing called mediumship. But, of course, we admit that they often come together."

Much of Manning's healing work is done through the mails, and he claims some "remarkable results." "You will no doubt consider us very unscientific," Manning says, "but our confessed approach is to *help people*. If we can also gather something that resembles proof along the way, so much the better.

"But I would rather see the patient *healed* believing that the doctor did it and that we were pure fakers, than to see some kind of delusion or partial healing that we might get 'credit' for.

"I really don't want to try to *sell* anybody or anything," Manning stresses. "We're strictly pragmatic about this. If something works for us we may use it for years before we feel we have time to consider *why* it works. And we probably learn more from our failures than from the successes."

Manning long dreamed of establishing a large research-service group which would be devoted to relatively "unscientific" research. A group of researchers would seek results first, then find the basic truths behind the work as revealed in the patterns of the accumulated successes. The ESP laboratory, a department of Spiritual Science Church 88, is the beginning of the physical manifestation of this dream.

"We do ask people for donations to share the cost of this help," Manning said. "Our books clearly show that we are *contributors* rather than beneficiaries of this work. Neither my wife, who is an excellent healer, nor I have ever received a penny for our time, and we regularly donate money to help seed the growth of the ESP Lab."

Al Manning made enough money in the business world to allow him and his wife to live in the relatively modest manner which they most enjoy.

"We do prefer to work with our 'patients' present so that we can physically direct the *light* through them by something akin to the laying on of hands." Manning stated, "but time and business have prevented us from doing much of that kind of work. When we have, we seem to get somewhat more spectacular results."

Curative Powers of the Blue Light

A sampling of testimonials to the benefits derived from the "Blue Light" of healing include:

"Yesterday I couldn't move a muscle," wrote N. W., of California. "Every inch of my body was sore, and I could not stand the touch of clothing. I couldn't lie down, and I couldn't stand up, and when I would try to walk I had to hold onto the wall for support because I was so shaky...I prayed for the Blue Light to surround me, to heal my mind and body. I asked forgiveness for my resentment, and in about thirty minutes, my mind became clear as a bell; my body did not hurt any more, and I felt strong, well, and happy...Thank you for your Blue Light and your help."

Manning pointed out that it was not good to interfere in the son's free choice regarding his drinking problem, but the ESP Laboratory would send him Light for spiritual growth that may bring him to choose a more uplifting path.

According to Manning, several of their truly "spectacular" healings will never appear in print, because they happened to highly respected businessmen who are "...deathly afraid that it might leak out that they are interested in these things and that it might hurt their business reputations."

The ESP Laboratory is unconcerned by the fact that they may never receive credit for these powerful demonstrations of their healing abilities. "As I said before," Manning says, "I'm not really selling anything. We're having a real ball helping people!"

"Love is the crowning grace of humanity, the holiest right of the soul, the golden link which binds us to duty and truth, like the redeeming principle that chiefly reconciles the heart of life, and is prophetic of eternal good." *Petrarch*

11

Love and Laughter Keep the Doctor Away

Who could resist loving a man like Henry Rucker, a spiritual healer who accepts what the great cosmic flow sends his way, a man who reacts to human need with warmth and love, a man who adjusts to trials and setbacks with a smile?

After listening to Henry deliver a talk to a standing-room-only audience, after watching him move gracefully about the platform, after observing the charisma of the healer, I teased him that sometimes he seemed like a combination of Bill Cosby and Father Divine. Henry takes his mission in life very seriously, but he is able to see the humor in his own humanity, and in his own struggles to achieve a spiritual balance.

Once, I heard several people give moving testimonials to Henry's remarkable abilities as a psychic healer. Then someone asked Henry if he is able to perform such techniques upon his own person. In that soft-voiced, deceptively deadpan delivery of his, Henry admitted that he could not. There were incredulous gasps of disbelief.

"Look, folks," Henry explained. "I love people and I feel for them, and I want to help. Thank God, some people I can help. The love energy flows through me. God does the healing. It's not old Henry doing the job. But somehow there is still a subjective element involved. I can't heal myself. When I've got a stomach ache, I take Bisodol. When I've got a headache, I take aspirin."

A Medical Doctor Tests Psychic Healers

Dr. C. Norman Shealy, a neurosurgeon with extremely impressive credentials (director of the Pain Rehabilitation Center, faculty member of both the University of Wisconsin and the University of Minnesota as Associate Clinical Professor of Neurosurgery, author or co-author of nearly ninety papers for professional journals, co-author of a recent book on unconventional healing) completed an extensive evaluation of Henry's healing ministry, together with those members of the Psychic Research Foundation who serve as healers. During a conversation with Dr. Shealy, I asked him specific questions related to Henry Rucker:

DR. C. NORMAN SHEALY: I walked into Henry's office in Chicago and he started to tell me about myself before I even sat down. He really did a fantastic reading on me. I spent three hours talking with Henry, and by the time I left I had an agreement with him that he would come to work with me on psychic diagnosis.

BRAD: Did you see Henry do any healing work in Chicago?

DR. SHEALY: No. But on the basis of his psychic reading of me I decided it would be worth working with him.

BRAD: Had you pre-selected patients for healing work?

DR. SHEALY: I didn't want to get into psychic healing at that point. I wanted only to work with matters that could be scientifically studied.

We brought seventeen patients down to my office. Each patient was brought into the room for only a few minutes. No questions by the psychics were allowed. We had previously taken samples of the patients' handwriting and their birth data, which were made available to the sensitives; but the psychics were afforded no opportunity to ask questions.

After each patient had left the room, I polled the eight psychic-sensitives. If they disagreed on something, I would say now let's vote on it. What do you all think? When we could get a consensus of six of them agreeing, I would write down the answer.

When we put it all together on personality and emotional problems, they were 98 per cent accurate. This is a fantastic record.

BRAD: By assessing the emotional state of the patient, do you mean the psychics judged whether the patient was depressed, elated, or nervous?

DR. SHEALY: Oh, the analyses were much deeper than that. The psychics provided elaborate discussions of the patients' family relationships, their marital problems, and so forth. Furthermore, they were 80 percent accurate on physical diagnoses.

BRAD: The physical diagnoses were specific?

DR. SHEALY: The psychics clearly gave the correct causes. Each patient's case was different. For instance, one was an accident victim, another was an attempted suicide, one was suffering from an infection, et cetera. The psychics got each one of them.

Furthermore, I took the psychics up to the ward to see patients who posed particular problems to therapy. The psychics only walked by the doors, and they were able to say such things as, "That man has a brain tumor and he will die." And he did!

BRAD: Was death expected in that case?

DR. SHEALY: Yes, we had expected death in his case. But the most baffling case I saw that weekend was a man in whom I had placed one of my dorsal-column stimulators two weeks before. The patient had become critically ill. His white blood count was almost fifty thousand. I thought that the shock of surgery had flared up latent leukemia that we had not known about.

Henry Rucker looked at the man and said, "This man does not have leukemia; he has liver failure."

I thought Henry had really goofed. But I had been out of town the day before the psychics arrived, and my assistant looked at me and said, "You know, he's right. Yesterday, while you were still out of town, we detected a very serious liver problem."

The patient still looked to me as if he was going to die. Henry waved his hands over the man—I don't know if he was healing him or not—and said: "This patient will be going home in ten days."

That was on Saturday. On Monday morning, I walked into the patient's room and he jumped out of bed and said: "Gee Doc, I feel great." I thought that was very impressive!

By the end of that weekend, I was convinced that psychics do an adequate job of diagnosis when they see patients in the flesh. Over the next couple of months, we decided to set up a research project utilizing clairvoyant diagnoses.

The plan was that I would send the psychics a photograph of a patient, a sample of his handwriting, a palm print, and his birth data. Then the specialists at Henry's Psychic Research Foundation would assess all these data and record their impressions.

Henry did about 180 patients himself, and his psychics at the foundation did about a hundred. This is how we recorded their clairvoyantly received impressions of the patients:

LOCATING SITE OF PAIN
Two clairvoyants . . . . 75% accurate
One clairvoyant 70%
Numerologist 60%
Astrologer 35%
Graphologist 25%

LOCATING CAUSE OF PAIN
Two clairvoyants . . . . 65% accurate
One clairvoyant 60%
All others . . . . 50% to 30%

BRAD: What kind of fee does Henry receive for this work?

DR. SHEALY: I pay Henry a very modest fee. Of course, I don't charge the patients anything for this. Almost without exception, the patients love Henry. I can think of only two who did not like him, and they were so severely psychologically disturbed that they hated everything. In general, my patients think that Henry is better than I am.

BRAD: How do you judge the effectiveness of a psychic healer—aside from the situation where the patient throws away his crutches and walks?

DR. SHEALY: Henry Rucker's interaction with some of my patients is not always something that I would say could be judged as healing. I look upon it largely as psychological counseling. I consider Henry Rucker to be the greatest psychologist that I have ever met!

BRAD: How would you rate Henry as a diagnostician?

DR. SHEALY: In his ability to assess emotional or personality problems, he is superb. From a physical point of view, he is reasonably good. On the basis of determining the site and the cause of pain from photographs, birth data, et cetera, the psychics at Henry's Psychical Research Foundation were getting about 75 percent accuracy, which is very good.

A Different Perspective

Before Henry became a professional psychic, he used to read palms because it was a way to meet people, to get to know them better. Then "Mr. Psychic," Clifford Royse, asked Henry to attend one of his psychic read-ins as a palmist. Henry was delighted—and a bit amazed—to find that people seemed to like his type of readings.

Knowing Reverend Royse gave Henry an opportunity to observe seances and mediumship. Later, he became acquainted with Joe East, who demonstrated automatic writing.

"My life was gaining full meaning for the first time," Henry recalls, "yet it was also becoming so very confusing. I had always had a fear of death, but these people were showing me that life did not end with the grave. I had always thought a lot about God, and now I was beginning to get a different perspective about the Father.

"I used to get these pictures of things in my head, and I was not able to understand what was happening. When nobody was around, I would talk to God and ask Him what

He wanted me to do. I knew He wanted me to do something, but I didn't know what it was. At that time, though, He wouldn't answer me. I used to shout at Him, 'I know you hear every word I say! Why won't you talk to me?'"

When Henry's parents used to take him to church as a child, he would squirm about in the pew with tears smarting his eyes. He wanted to be a part of the Church, but he could not accept the dogma of hell and damnation. He could not conceive of a God that would make him frail and weak, then punish him for his ignorance and his lack of strength. When he began getting "pictures" through his psi faculties, his fundamental religious background set up an internal warfare that raged within Henry's psyche for years.

"Way back in 1944, when I was in the Army," Henry remembered, "a wrinkled-up little Filipino, who seemed as old as the hills, gave me a reading. I believe he must have been relaying a message from God. At the time, the old guy really frightened me, because the things he told me seemed so ominous. Nevertheless, I was fascinated by what he said. I kept the things he said in mind, and I decided that I would do palmistry the way he did."

In the mid-1970s, Henry returned to the Philippines, and became fast friends with Dr. Tony Agpaoa, one of the more famous of the controversial psychic surgeons.

"I know that there have been a lot of negative things said about Dr. Tony," Henry remarked. "Tony realized years ago that many bad things will happen to many of us in this field. We are going to be called phonies, we are going to be called black magicians and persecuted."

Henry had always felt that he could heal people, but he had been reluctant to claim to be a channel for such sharing of the love energy. But then Tony consecrated Henry's hands.

"This is the thing that really brought my life into focus," Henry affirms. "My psychic awareness has been greatly stimulated by my healing work. Tony also gave me a talisman, which I cherish. There is something special about it. It has a lot of magnetic power in it."

Bridging the Gap

It is Henry's objective as director of the Psychic Research Foundation to bridge the gaps that currently exist between theology, science, and metaphysics.

"I am black, but I am a Westerner in this life, and therefore I am an activist. I want to stay involved with life. I want to turn on and turn others on and be a light. I don't want to just *hold* the light, you see; I want to *be* it, become *one* with it.

"My own personal satisfaction is in knowing that I am doing what I am supposed to be doing. My pleasure is in seeing the things manifest that I have been told about. Prominence and popularity are not nearly as important as seeing myself doing things that I know God would have me do.

"Our concepts of religion or philosophy are but measuring sticks to guide us. No matter where we are born, God provides us with these measuring sticks. If we were born in the Eastern countries, our concept of God would be quite different from that of the people of the West. But all views of God are valid. All these different roads lead to one point. There are only outward differences, and they are only semantic. The differences among religions are only the differences of language and interpretation. All religions are saying the same thing: there is something *outside* and, at the same time, inside of you; and you are an extension of this force."

A Vehicle for the Love Force

I have always been intrigued by the way in which Henry and his co-workers at the Psychical Research Foundation employ certain African dialects in some of their healing work.

"The particular dialect we use is not important," Henry explained. "We use these dialects in our healing work because we can control powers which are not known by ordinary individuals. We use them to change the vibrations in a place. By intoning certain vibrations, I can change people's concepts. By chanting, I could change vibrations in this room so that a person wouldn't want to walk through the door. I don't do demonstrations like that just to show off or to prove a point, however."

Henry does not perform idle demonstrations of psychic prowess to impress the gullible. "I just want people who might be influenced by me to be able to see life with a different set of values. I want my fellow man to know that he and God have been one since he has been. I'm only a talented vehicle for the healing work. That belongs entirely to God."

Removing Negativity with Love

It is difficult to receive an effective healing if you feel blocked by negativity. Here is a technique that I have used with great success over the years.

Let us say that you have been bombarded with negativity by a vicious person or by a situation that has left you feeling rather defeated and very much alone in the world. Perhaps you are away from home, and you feel that everyone in that strange environment is against you.

Go to your room or to a place where you can re-establish your emotional and spiritual equilibrium. Sit quietly for a moment. If possible, play some soft, restful music. It is always a good idea to travel with your cassette player and a number of New Age music albums in your suitcase.

After you have begun to calm yourself, say, as you *inhale*, "I am." On the *out breath*, say, "relaxed."

Repeat this process a number of times. Take comfortably deep breaths: "I am," asserting your sovereignty and your individual reality on the intake; "relaxed" positively affirming your calm condition on the out breath.

Now visualize someone who is extremely positive, who loves you, and who shares your philosophy, your perspective, your point of view about life and the cosmos. This may be a spouse, a friend, a business associate, a teacher.

See the person on whom you are focusing turning toward you with a smile of love. See the person extending his or her hand to yours.

Feel the touch of fingertip to fingertip. Sense the electrical crackle of energy moving between you. Experience the warmth of the love that flows from entity to entity.

Visualize yourself taking that person's hand in your own. Feel comfortable knowing that there is one who loves you and who exhibits concern for you.

See this shared love erecting a barrier between you and the negative bombardment to which you have been subjected that day.

Next image you or your friend reaching forth a hand to take another's. Visualize yet another like-minded man or woman who is being welcomed to your circle. See that person joining you, smiling as he or she takes a place beside you to add to your fortress of bonded energy.

Continue to imagine other men and women joining your circle until you have built as large a barrier of love as you feel that you need to face the hostility or the negativity that is being directed against you in this strange and unfamiliar environment. Feel strength, born of love, swell within your breast.

Visualize love energy moving from member to member of your magic circle. See the Golden Light of Protection encircling your group externally. See the energy of unconditional love flowing from one to another as you imagine yourself holding hands and linking your vibratory frequency to that of others of your spiritual philosophy.

After you have seen and felt the love energy moving among your circle, visualize the ultraviolet light of the Source of All-That-Is descending from above and touching each of your members on the crown chakra. Feel yourself vibrating with the greatest emanation of love from the very heart of the Universe.

Hold this image and this energy as long as is needed.

When you have become completely fortified and calmed, it is best to go to bed and enjoy a peaceful night's rest. If this is impossible and you must return to the difficult environment, know that you will do totally prepared and reinforced for any situation which might arise. Stride confidently into the "arena," knowing that you are linked together in an unbreakable bond of love with those kindred souls who share your perspective and your goals.

"Either we have an immortal soul, or we have not. If we have not, we are beasts; the first and wisest of beasts it may be, but still beasts. We only differ in degree, and not in kind—just as an elephant differs from the slug. But by the concession of the materialists, we are not of the same kind as beasts; and this also we say from our own consciousness. Therefore, methinks it must be the possession of a soul within us that makes the difference." *Coleridge*

12

Developing Your "Extra Special Powers"

For the past ten years, Sucile Lujan, a psychic sensitive with a strong social conscience, has been using her ESP to cure young people of their addiction to drugs and alcohol.

"Many times I pick up a drug problem with a child when I am reading for the parents," stated Mrs. Lujan, a respected Phoenix, Arizona sensitive. "I see clearly that the child is into drugs or alcohol, and I present this information to my clients.

"Sometimes they argue that this cannot be so in their family, but I continue to pick up on so many specifics that they believe me. In some cases, I have clairvoyantly seen a child as young as twelve completely hooked on cocaine."

Sucile said that for some reason she is so sensitive to people with drug dependency problems that she doesn't even have to be "reading" for them. "The word 'drugs' will just flash on and off over their heads in multicolored lights like those on a Christmas tree."

Ms. Lujan explained that once she has impressed the parents with her ability to tune in on a sensitive family situation, they usually make arrangements for her to do a reading for their child.

"Many times I pick up impressions that go back to when the child was only five or six. Most problems that lead to later addiction begin right in the home. In some cases the child was abused and made to feel inferior. In other instances, the parents themselves at that time were recreational drug users and saw nothing wrong in freely smoking marijuana or sniffing cocaine in front of the child."

In some cases, a parent's ill-advised choice of words to a young child sowed the seeds for later addiction.

"One father would always say 'You're no son of mine,' when the boy would get into minor troubles, like snitching a cookie or spilling a glass of milk. The man said those words so often to his son as the boy was maturing that the child eventually came to fear that he was illegitimate and that his father did not claim him. Feelings of inferiority led the boy to become a drug addict."

Sucile begins young people with drug or alcohol problems on a twice-a-week schedule. During their appointment times she teaches them how to use meditation and creative visualization rather than drugs. It usually requires no more than three months of such meetings to cure the children of their addiction.

"I get them to start looking forward, not backward. I teach them how to meditate and to visualize good things coming in their lives. The kids get a natural high from meditation and it isn't long before they are telling me that the natural high is far superior to that which they formerly achieved through drugs."

As part of the curative technique, Sucile assists the children in creating tapes that will reprogram their minds. "The children use their own voices to repeat the positive suggestions. They choose their own kind of music to serve as a dramatic background score to their personal program of therapy."

The kids soon discover that Sucile's remarkable psychic abilities will always let her know if they fall back into dependency on drugs or alcohol.

"They quickly find out that they cannot fool me or lie to me. If they do backslide, I help them determine the reason why they are holding on to their addiction."

Sucile sadly admits that there are instances when a child is so heavily addicted and so unhappy in the world that he or she will choose suicide rather than surrender the drug dependency or make any effort to cure the problem.

"Usually this has occurred in situations where there was so little parental love and the children had so little self esteem that they simply rejected the choice to improve themselves. In one such instance, the spirit of the boy came to me and spoke through me to his mother and assured her that he was much happier in the spirit world. He had simply not wanted to be in the physical, earth plane world."

Sucile also recognizes the possibility of spirit possession in certain cases of drug or alcohol dependency.

"I believe that low-level entities can enter certain people when they are under the influence of drugs or alcohol. Many individuals have claimed to have seen ugly, demonic-type beings when they were drinking.

"I've talked to some kids who say that being under the control of drugs is sometimes like being lost in a dark jungle with all kinds of hideous creatures after them.

"It is also interesting to me to observe that since most drinking or drug-taking is done in groups, the negative, possessing entities seem always to pursue the weakest member of a gathering."

Sucile Lujan is emphatic in advising serious drug counsel for young children. "They must early learn the unfortunate consequences of the recreational use of drugs."

She also feels strongly that psychologists and psychiatrists should take courses in psychic development. "They need to be able to teach their patients how to meditate. They need to have the knowledge of how to regress a patient back to the time when the problem first began."

There is no question in Sucile Lujan's mind that ESP can help salvage lives that would have been lost to the nightmarish world of drug abuse.

Stretching Your Psychic Muscles

So often people who are just beginning to develop their ESP abilities expect to *see* clear and distinct images at once. Sometimes, especially when you are just developing, you will *feel*, rather than see something. You will seem to feel that something will occur at six o'clock. You will feel that your aunt is trying to contact you. You will feel that you should not board that particular airplane and take that particular flight.

Seeing often comes later, after your psychic muscles have become much better developed.

Beginning Experiments with Telepathy

Telepathy, as you no doubt understand, simply means that a person can make contact with another through the mind.

When you experiment with telepathy for the first time, you may find to your surprise that you soon hear from someone whom you have been thinking about, almost as if that person knew you want to hear from him or her.

If you deliberately set out to "reach" someone via your mental telephone, you may encounter a delay in receiving a *physical* response. This should not discourage you; you will "know" that the telepathic message reached its destination if you feel a mental response at the time.

If you are visualizing the recipient of your message clearly and you suddenly feel a small tingle in you arm or your solar plexus, then you will know that your message has been received on some level of the person's consciousness. You don't have to imagine this response, for it will be real enough.

Usually it is best to sit quietly for a few moments before attempting a telepathic transfer.

Visualize the vastness of space. Contemplate the meaningless of time.

See yourself as a circle that grows and grows until it

occupies the Earth, the galaxy. See yourself blending into a Oneness with All-That-Is.

Now visualize the one whom you wish to contact. See him or her plainly. Feel the other person's presence.

In your mind, speak to this person as if he or she were sitting there before you. Do not speak aloud. Speak mentally.

Breathe in comfortably deep breaths, for this will give added power to the broadcasting station of the psyche.

Mentally relay the message which you wish your friend or loved one to receive from you. Ask him or her to call you or get in touch with you.

Transmitting Healing Thoughts

You may also send healing thoughts to those who are ill. You must understand, of course, that it is not you who heals, but your act of tuning in to the Infinite Mind which does so.

If someone is bereaved, you may send him or her a comforting thought that the Divine Will has been done and that It will soon send solace.

If you are concerned about someone who has a bad habit that needs correcting, you may send mental pictures to that individual which show him/her hating that habit so much that s/he freely chooses to give it up.

When you send healing thoughts to those who are ill, you must visualize those people as being completely healed. You must not permit yourself to see them as they are at the present time: miserable in the throes of their illnesses. You must actually see these individuals in the desired state of health and *know* that it will be so.

When you picture your subjects, who are plagued with bad habits, they, too, must be seen as triumphant over their problems. You must visualize them as having completely forsaken the habit. Only by seeing those bad habits as negated will they be discontinued.

The most vital point in telepathically healing or helping is this: You must actually *see* the desired conditions and *know* that it will be so.

If you wish to learn how a certain person really feels about you, make yourself a receiving set for his or her thoughts.

Sit quietly and breathe slowly in comfortably deep breaths.

Picture in your mind that this particular person is sitting or standing there before you, and ask him or her: "What do you really think of me?"

If you receive a very warm gentle impulse or tingle, you will immediately know that the person in question likes you. If you receive a cool impulse, the person in question may dislike you or may be deceitful in dealing with you.

Developing Psychic Powers

Experiments with Olof Jonsson

One night I was working some ESP experiments with Olof Jonsson, the psychic who participated with Astronaut Ed Mitchell in the Moon-to-Earth experiment in telepathic transfer. Olof is perhaps the most powerful physical sensitive in the world today. Under laboratory conditions he has "guessed" correctly 100 percent of the time in run after run with the Zener ESP testing cards—the cross, the square, the wavy line, the circle, and the star. I personally have witnessed Olof materialize and de-materialize objects, and make tables dance across rooms.

Olof suggests that beginners seeking to develop their "unknown sensory perception" try such elementary exercises as guessing people's birthdays. "It's not *extra*," Olof insists. "Only *unknown* at the present time." Try to tune in on what friends might have been doing during the day. Or, you can throw dice and try to guess what numbers will come up. You might try dealing cards at random from a deck, then toss them face down, and attempt to guess their value."

According to Olof:

"Erase everything from your mind. Forget all about those petty things that are troubling you and relax your mind.

Attain peace and calm.

Achieve harmony.

Do not think!

You must release the irritations in your mind and banish all things that disturb you.

You must tell yourself to become calm and peaceful.

You must command yourself to react to no outside distractions. Once you have achieved the proper conditions, you will feel psychic energy and *knowing* build up within you.

Do not think! That is the difference between the way your conscious and your unconscious minds work.

You must remain absolutely calm at the time your unconscious is controlling your actions.

Mind-Linking

It is difficult for me to develop an excitement about guessing Zener cards, but I wanted to mind-link with Olof and work the cards with him.

I created a device for non-thought: I concentrated on an enormous snow bank, and endless expanse of white. After I had retained this image for a few moments, there came a certain "knowing" that told me that I could draw a star from the deck. I did so.

"Now a circle," Olof said.

I withdrew a circle. I was finding it easier to blank out my conscious thoughts. I would let my mind go blank, then keep shuffling and shuffling until my mind just seemed to move to its own volition and pick out the card I visualized.

"Isn't it a wonderful feeling when the knowing comes?" Olof asked me.

I readily agreed. "It is a strange feeling, but it is definitely not a *thinking*. You receive an image, say, of the circle; and you go shuffle...shuffle...shuffle...then, pop! There it is."

The mental conditions had to be totally right for the next experiment.

After we had shuffled the deck thoroughly, Olof asked me to draw five cards at random from the complete deck of ESP cards. When I had blindly selected my five cards, Olof quickly withdrew five cards of his own. Then, with the cards held behind our backs, we withdrew one card at a time and matched four out of five!

Imagine the odds against such a rumpling of the laws of chance. Two men had selected two sets of four out of five cards that matched in a random selection, then, without knowledge of those cards, had brought them out from behind their backs in matching sequence, four out of five times!

Olof has another method of developing psychic abilities to share with those who may one day wish to expand their psychic prowess:

Fill a glass of water and place it on the table before you. Stare at the water for five minutes or so, and erase all thoughts from your mind. Do not think of a thing. Just look at the water.

Once you feel that you have achieved the proper conditions, practice guessing cards from an ESP deck. The glass of water is merely a physical object on which to focus your attention and to permit the unconscious mind to rise above your conscious mind. Once you have learned to blank out your conscious mind by concentrating on the glass of water, you will find it easier to achieve the altered-state-of-consciousness for the exercise to your psychic abilities.

How to Read Objects

The famous psychometrist, Dorothy Spence Lauer, once shared with me the following exercise for encouraging your ability to "read" objects:

When you first begin to psychometrize an article, such as a hairpin, letter, or earring, speak spontaneously. Do not hesitate to say exactly what comes to your mind.

There is no need to concentrate, or even to think hard; in fact, the secret lies in just being spontaneous, immediately saying what comes to you. This can be a little embarrassing, if something of a very intimate nature should come to you, but if you truly feel the urge to speak frankly, you should do so.

You may begin by psychometrizing for yourself. Take an object that belongs to you, something that you have worn or used for some time, such as a comb or a ring.

Sit quietly, holding the object.

Do not force ideas or concentrate.

Have a pad and pencil at your side, and as fast as your thoughts come to you, write them down. There will be times when you will say, "This sounds impossible"; still, write it all down. Do not continue this exercise for too long a period, however.

By psychometrizing for yourself, you will find that you have received insights which can guide you in your daily life. Infinite intelligence can channel through you at this time.

Do not take credit for this information or become egotistical in your work. Remember the words from the *Bible*: "I, of myself, can do nothing."

The power that guides you will disappear if you become smug and arrogant. You must remember that you are an instrument tuned to receive.

When you psychometrize for other persons, you may tell them your impressions rather than jotting them down. To further experiment and to increase your psychometric abilities, ask friends to loan you their old letters from people whom you do not know. Request objects which they have received through family inheritances, and so forth. Remember that you are an instrument, and permit the messages to flow through you in a spontaneous manner.

Here are some psychic responses that I have noticed in my own readings which may be applicable in yours:

Should you suddenly feel a headache that you did not have before, this may be an indication that the person with whom you are working is troubled with headaches. Advise the person to see a physician, then clear yourself by visualizing a violet, healing light cleansing you.

If you have the feeling of something falling, advise the person to be careful of an object which could fall on him.

If you feel that you are riding in an automobile or an airplane, it may mean that the person is going to travel.

If you feel that you should be cautious of words, tell the person to be careful of what she says in business negotiations.

The Goal and Meaning of Life

OLOF JONSSON: When a person has nothing to believe in beyond himself and exists only for material acquisitions, things are not as they should be. When personal selfishness has become a religion, spiritual danger is unavoidable. Personal selfishness spawns violence between individuals and war between nations.

All the techniques of our modern technology seem to push on faster and faster, perhaps only toward a vacuum which lies in readiness for us in the stockpiles of nuclear armaments.

Civilized man is in the process of losing his soul. A spiritual undermining has long been at work, so that it is no longer in vogue to believe in something.

Throughout the ages, the faith that sustained man sprung not out of materialism and easy living, but out of hardship and pain. The person who is forced to fight his way through suffering somehow becomes supplied with strength.

The orthodox, organized churches have taken little responsibility toward investigating the Unknown levels of spirituality and achieving Cosmic Harmony with the Universe. They have become entirely too worldly and more concerned with the careful administration of their property holdings and their business affairs than the ministry of basic spiritual principles.

It is not the big, well-organized mass meetings that will give modern man the directions to the paths of life and death. Here and there in our nation and elsewhere in the world, there are groups of people in small, obscure movements, who are seeking to find the meaning of existence and the secret of immortality.

The power of mind that lies within each man is capable of working miracles when it takes a good and right course, but it can also be destructive when it is ruled by the power of evil sustained by a spirit of personal selfishness and an obsession with materialism.

Perhaps the true purpose of the spiritual life is to offer help and comfort to the suffering, concern for the weak, and good will and unselfish acts to everyone.

No man needs to be afraid of dying. The order of Nature, the Cosmic Harmony of the Universe tells us that in all forms of existence, everything has meaning, nothing comes about by chance. It is blasphemous to believe that man alone should be excluded from the orderliness and purposefulness of the Universe. The secret of life's course and death's chambers is found within each of us in the unknown levels of the unconscious, wherein lie many dormant powers.

The utilization of the powers, the "sparks of divinity," within each of us, should never tempt the wise to make a religion out of spiritual blessings that have been dispensed to all men. Rather, an awareness of the powers within should serve to equip the interested and the receptive with a brilliant searchlight on the path to Cosmic Harmony.

It is in one's own home, in his own little chamber, in moments of quiet meditation that a stream of the great light of Cosmos is best able to reach in and enrich the soul and open the eyes to the magnificent and tranquil gardens that lie beyond the borders of the Unknown. That which governs a man's life is neither chemistry, nor physics, nor anything material, but the proper spiritual link up with the powers within his own psyche and the blessed Harmony that governs the Universe.

13

Health and the Stars

H. Douglas Miller of Detroit is an articulate, college-educated astrologer. He became a full-fledged practitioner of the "mother of sciences" when he received his certificate from the American Federation of Astrologers in Washington, D.C. I had read and heard that many astrologers and medical doctors believe that there is a definite correlation between the Moon and certain health problems. For example, ulcer patients are said to suffer more bleeding during the time of the full Moon; patients undergoing surgery also have been noted to bleed more profusely at this time.

To answer some of the questions concerning an astrologer's approach to healing, I decided to talk with Miller.

BRAD: Is there such a thing as "medical" astrology?

MILLER: In astrology, the different planets exert their separate and distinct influences in terms of life in general, and for our purpose here, in terms of the working of the animal organism.

The Sun has a vitalizing influence.

Mars has an irritating or inflammatory influence.

Saturn emits a restricting or hindering influence.

Mercury has a variable influence, with special reference to the nervous system.

Jupiter affects growth and has a special influence on the liver.

The Moon has a special rulership over the fluids in the body.

BRAD: It sounds complicated.

MILLER: It is, but it is based on simple principles. If we have a horoscope, we logically approach each of the planets with a view to adding up the different values related to the planets, as I have just described.

BRAD: Can you give an example of a specific case?

MILLER: Certainly. I once told a client that I believed her mother would have to watch out for a painful inflammation in the region of the lower digestive tract. I was able to predict this due to the fact that I saw a badly conditioned planet (Mars: inflammation, heat, pain) in the zodiacal sign Virgo (large and small intestine) about to receive some stress in the near future by what we call progression.

Progression means the advent of new planetary energies which modify the influence of the energies which were in the chart of the person at the time and place of birth.

The client said that her doctor saw no trouble of the sort that I had described. She insisted that I must be wrong. She insisted that her mother had gall bladder trouble and nothing else.

Two or three days after the time that I stated would be most liable to cause her mother health trouble, the woman had a acute attack of appendicitis.

BRAD: That seems to be hitting the mark rather closely.

MILLER: I could cite several other cases in point. For example, at the very day on which a client of mine admitted developing multiple sclerosis, the planets indicated exactly the sort of breakdown of nerve tissue which would produce the condition.

BRAD: Does the horoscope usually speak so specifically?

MILLER: No, it is generally not quite so graphic. It is more likely to give a person the etiology of a disease rather than to speak of the surface symptoms.

BRAD: I think most people consider one's horoscope to indicate such things as marriage, job advancement and accidents of a physical nature. Is there really that much medical information to be derived from a reading of the horoscope?

MILLER: Horoscopes speak in medical terms so often that it behooves the astrologer to do quite a bit of reading to keep up with what the charts are trying to say. Horoscopes are like serial x-rays. They show you what has led up to the present health picture and what will result from it. In so doing, they also give the astrologer some valuable clues as to what needs to be done. Very often, the report of the client's doctor will confirm what the astrologer believes to be the trouble.

BRAD: Astrologers would not prescribe medicine for clients, though, would they?

MILLER: Of course not. The astrologer does not prescribe medicines or give advice like a regular physician, but often an astrologer acts as a good trouble-shooter.

BRAD: How might an astrologer best serve a client in conjunction with the services of a medical doctor?

MILLER: One of the best functions of the astrologer in the field of medicine lies in setting up what are called 'elections' or times for having operations or for commencing treatment. Few people do not believe in the wisdom of waiting for the proper election.

The astrologer chooses a time for operating when the star picture most favors the person's health rulers in the horoscope. The astrologer fortifies these rulers as much as possible and chooses the best planetary hour for the operation.

One of the most inviolable of rules is not to operate on that part of the body in which the Moon is posited at the time of the operation or in the sign opposite to it.

BRAD: Does the Moon really have a great deal of influence on the body processes?

MILLER: A few years ago, a ball player was reported to be in need of corrective surgery on his foot. I remarked that this was a bad time for the operation, but no one made any mention to the athlete of the great peril to his health.

Complications developed, and shortly thereafter, surgeons were compelled to operate again. The man became feverish and died.

In the one case, the operation took place when the transitting Moon was in Pisces, which governs the feet, and thus violated the rule. The second operation occurred when the Moon was in Virgo, the sign opposite Pisces.

BRAD: Do you feel that such instances are common?

MILLER: If you were to check the time when operations were performed which led to post-operative complications and compared them with twenty times their accompanying election horoscopes when the operations produced good, long-term results, you could not help being impressed with the contrast between the star patterns in the one set of instances as compared to the other. The evidence is overwhelming to those who would make an unbiased examination.

14

Long-Distance Medical Diagnosis

Some years ago, I conducted a most impressive series of experiments in long-distance clairvoyance with the late British seer, John Pendragon.

I knew that Pendragon required several lines of handwriting, a recent photograph, and full birth data from each of his clients. I gave him none of these things, and nothing to work from other than my signature at the bottom of typed letters. Yet over the span of three thousand miles, a firm bond developed between us.

In a letter of December 1st, 1966, John Pendragon added, almost as an afterthought: "One thing I meant to have written weeks ago. Clairvoyantly I get that you have some relatively minor trouble cooking up in your left leg, below the knee. Something is building up here. Are you varicose-veined? No need to get rattled."

Well, I did not have varicose veins, but upon examining my left leg below the knee, I was less than pleased to spot a small bump. My doctor noted that it was just a vein bulging out a bit. Nothing to be worried about.

Pendragon was pleased that he had "hit" my leg without the help of my horoscope, photo, or any bond other than my typed letters. "Note the doc agrees with me that it is nothing to get nervous about. I wonder what he would say if he knew I had 'seen' your leg at several thousand miles?"

Then, in the same letter, he asked: "Shall I have a shot at your wife (Marilyn, who died in 1982)? I feel that she is concerned about some mild gynecological trouble. Again, no cause for alarm. She also seems over-concerned about her weight."

In Marilyn's case, Pendragon did not even have the weak bond of typewritten letters to link his mind to hers. Pendragon's letter was posted from England on December 8th, 1966. On that very day, in our doctor's office in Iowa, my wife sat discussing both of the matters Pendragon had described.

Perhaps the most dramatic domestic episode was foreseen by Pendragon on January 16, 1967, when, in a 100-percent accurate clairvoyant reading, without any personal object to constitute a bond, he predicted that Marilyn was about to break one of her "foot springs."

On February 14, Marilyn broke her foot while playing paddle-ball with—of all people—our doctor's wife. Marilyn, who had always been good-naturedly open-minded about my research into the world of the paranormal, lost a large share of her skepticism on that particular Valentine's Day.

An interesting demonstration of prophecy and the nature of time was afforded us on March 29, 1967, when Pendragon wrote to warn us about a slight rash that would appear on the legs and arms of one of our children.

"This will not be due to an allergy or virus, but appears due to some irritant," he wrote. "Not serious. *Might be past condition, but think it future.*"

I do not wish to inject technical data at this point, but time, to a clairvoyant, seems to be an Eternal Now and requires great sensitivity to determine if an envisioned event lies in the future or in the past. The point is, in this case, that our younger son had had the envisioned rash about three weeks before Pendragon's letter. To Pendragon, the rash had seemed a future event. In reality, the experience was a part of our immediate past—which does not in any way minimize the fact that Pendragon received a clairvoyant impression of that rash, although separated from us by three thousand miles.

Pendragon Explains How He Does It

When I am in good psychic form and properly tuned in, I could get impressions while standing on my head. However, I do employ a kind of technique for map-reading.

I like to have a picture frame about twelve inches by eighteen inches filled with black paper or dull-finished black fabric—a sort of "black projection screen," rather like a negative cinema screen. I find that the screen also helps in receiving clairvoyant impressions other than those connected with my map-dowsing, but it does not put me off not to have it.

I prop the screen up in front of my typewriter if I propose to type as I see the "film." If the machine comes between me and the picture in an obstructive sense—and it sometimes does—then I just watch the "film" first and type what I have seen after the images have stopped coming. The mechanics of typing do occasionally disturb me, but much depends on how attuned I am.

I explore the map with a finger—usually the forefinger of my right hand—and what I am touching on the map usually projects itself onto the screen. I find that for best results I must be free of emotion and personal worries. I must be calmly poised. I also find that I must not try. A rather indifferent attitude appears to be best. If I knit brows and get anxious, the picture either will not come or if it does, I lose it.

I sometimes use a steel knitting needle as a pointer. A pencil will do, also, but my forefinger is the best.

I like a small-scale map to start with. If, let us say, I should put my finger on a small town in Kansas, I might take a map of the town itself and run my forefinger up and down the main street, receiving detailed impressions of various buildings, concentrating on various sites.

I emphasize that I do not need the screen as a physical crutch in my map-dowsing work. The picture can appear in mid-air. On occasion, there may be no picture at all, but simply a subjective impression.

Medical Readings

PENDRAGON: In doing medical readings for people, I use the screen less often. Medically, I get my best results without seeing the person physically.

Subjectively, I saw Brad Steiger's leg lump at a distance of over three thousand miles. If he had been with me physically, I might not have got it at all. I tend to get put off by seeing the person physically. Too many sensorial stimuli are being activated.

Of course, I do get medical information about people when I see them physically. I also "see" a sort of highly complex pattern, which if I attempted to explain it to the person, would probably elicit a response of, "But I am not like that at all!"

That is because I see the *real* person—all of the person. I see the child, the adolescent, the adult who is before me, and the future person, all rolled into one. The difficulty lies in separating the past from the future. The *how* eludes me in most cases, but it is obvious the spiritual, psychological, and physical person are all blended.

Projecting Astrally

PENDRAGON: I feel that the psychic talent of astral projection is closely allied to long-distance clairvoyance. I can project myself astrally, but not in the fashion of the highly colored and imaginative works I have read on the subject. I have no technique to explain. Indeed, I do not know how I do it. It just seems to work. I project myself so easily and see so many things in various parts of the world, both in time and space, that I cannot always tell where they are or prove each instance.

On June 6, 1967, I wrote Brad Steiger's name on a note pad and put my finger on it. In a few seconds, I found myself upstairs in his Iowa home.

It was nighttime. I could hear the fussy cries of a young child and the anxious voices of Brad and his wife. I got that their younger daughter was upset, but her condition was not as serious as the parent's solicitude indicated. By an effort of will, I drew myself back to England and went directly to the typewriter.

Briefly, I described the situation I had witnessed, then told the Steigers: "I get that your little girl has unsuspected indigestion. I see her vomiting. This is due to undigested milk and milk products which form an undigested mass in the stomach. Does she gulp milk? Milk, especially cold, can be indigestible. Put a pinch of bicarbonate of soda or a bit of fizzy soda water into her milk. Nothing to get anxious about, but it could lay the seeds of a chronic state. I do feel she is gulping and needs watching in this respect."

Brad wrote back that I had "once again struck a bull's-eye." Their daughter was in the habit of gulping her milk, and they had lately taken to giving her a cold bottle of milk at bedtime. The scene I had witnessed had not culminated in any serious illness, but the Steigers told me that their daughter's discomfort had returned on the next few evenings, because they had persisted in allowing her to gulp cold milk at bedtime. "After your letter arrived," Brad said "my wife tried adding the pinch of bicarb. The last two nights, our daughter has slept without discomfort and without awakening."

"I am fully convinced that the soul is indestructible, and that its activity will continue through eternity. It is like the sun, which to our eyes, seems to set at night; but it has in reality only gone to diffuse its light elsewhere." *Goethe*

15

Soul Projection

The five-year-old boy lay burning with fever. What had begun as a chest cold had developed into an acute case of pleurisy, and the boy's lungs were rapidly filling with the fluid that would gradually extinguish his life force.

"Daddy," the boy moaned. "Please bring me a drink...so thirsty..."

"Your daddy is across the ocean," his stepmother told the boy gently. "I'll bring you a drink."

The woman left the boy's sick room in a state of agitation. She did not know how to cope with such a situation. The doctor had told her that the boy hovered on the edge of death, that this night might be his last. What could she do other than to maintain a vigil at his bedside and pray for his recovery?

Her daughter approached her in the kitchen where she was filling a glass with fresh water. "How is little Paul?" the girl asked.

"He's no better...worse," the woman said, catching nervously at her lower lip with her teeth. "The doctor came while you were in school today. He said that Paul may die."

The woman barely managed to release the final word before she burst into tears. What could she do to help the boy? What would her new husband think of her if she allowed his young son to die?

Her daughter was strangely calm. "There is a way," she said. "There is a way to help Paul."

"If you know a way, then help him!" her mother screamed, dangerously near hysteria.

"I shall," the girl said matter-of-factly.

Late that night, the girl slipped into her young stepbrother's room.

"They say that tonight is likely to be your last, little Paul," she whispered as she paused beside the bed where the boy lay. "I shall not allow that to happen."

The girl sat down beside the bed and assumed the lotus posture. She took a couple of deep breaths and slipped out of her physical form into the *Atma Sarup,* the soul body.

In her non-physical self, she was removed from the normal barriers of time and space. She took the boy out of his physical body, also, and the two soul bodies hung off the ceiling, viewing the body on the bed below.

"See, Paul," his stepsister pointed out, "your astral body is like a large x-ray of your human form. Do not be alarmed and do not be frightened."

Years later, Paul recalled that his stepsister accomplished his healing by impressing upon both his astral and his physical body the thought that he would be made whole again.

"Instantly, I knew that all was well and that the living clay lying on the bed would be my temple again. However, I was reluctant to go back into the body. It seemed so wonderful to be able to soar free of the flesh. But my stepsister impressed upon me the thought that it was necessary to return to the human body.

"The next moment I remember awakening to find the family standing by the bed, completely surprised at the swift recovery of their youngest child. Two weeks later when my father returned home, I heard him thank my stepsister for saving my life; it seemed that he had projected himself to the house, from overseas, for the same reason, only to find my stepsister taking care of it."

To the late Paul Twitchell, who became the controversial ECK master, such a method of healing was one of the oldest arts. He stated that many saints healed through the use of the soul body.

Twitchell taught the ancient science of controlled bilocation, or soul travel. In order to become a member of the secret world brotherhood that uses this facility of being able to get in and out of the body to heal others even at a distance, Twitchell claimed that he and his stepsister studied under Sudar Singh in Allahabad, India. Later, Twitchell found Rebazar Tarzs, the great Tibetan Lama, who was teaching Eckankar.

"But healing is only one aspect of Eckankar," Twitchell stressed. "Its primary purpose is to give the soul an opportunity to travel the ancient, secret path to the true realm of God."

Testimonials to Absentee Healing

Twitchell's daily mail was flooded with requests for help and testimonials to previous healings:

From Mrs. H. R., in Nevada: "...I was in bed and the conviction that I would be made whole came as if out of nowhere, as my mind was not consciously concerned with the state of my health. This strong conviction stayed with me for hours and as I said, my improvement has been constant since. Again thanks for your help and may it continue."

From Miss M. R., Denver, Colorado: "Just talked with J. G. You did it again! She is talking almost perfectly. Still an occasional scratchiness, but she is so very much better...you are magnificent!"

A testimonial from West Germany: "I was very skeptical...a good beginning has been achieved and I am longing for my complete recovery. Therefore I beg you to continue your efforts in healing my appalling illness of muscular dystrophy. At the same time I thank you very much for all the goodness I'll be lucky to receive from the spiritual gift of healing."

One might argue that much of the adept's power lay in auto-suggestion. This may or may not be true, but what made this one man such a charismatic figure that he could inspire healing at distances of several thousand miles? What was there about the rather anonymous personality of Paul Twitchell that was so commanding? Or did his soul body, the *Atma Sarup,* actually transcend the laws of time and space and aid the natural laws of healing?

From N. K., New Jersey: "I'd like to begin with thanks...so thanks so much for healing my fluttering, afflicted heart. I felt your healing."

From I. K., England: "My husband has noticed light at the sides of his eyes. Our first real sign of improvement in years." (Then, in a follow-up letter four months later) "I am happy to say that the light coming in at the sides of his eyes has now clarified to allow him to discern shapes."

From I. B., England: "I wrote to you in January to ask for your help. Having had five operations, I was desperate. Now after three years, I am well after receiving your letters. I have had no return of my illness."

On and on the letters came, and Twitchell gave me unlimited access to his correspondence. Students and former patients of Twitchell testify to his ability to heal via the soul body and to read the Akashic records of former incarnations, in which, many believe, the true origin of illness in the present life may be found.

A Dialogue about Healing

Several questions come to the mind of the skeptic and the searcher alike. In an early interview, I allowed Paul Twitchell to answer them for himself.

BRAD: How does absentee healing work?

TWITCHELL: One must remember that healing of this nature is such an intricate process that those who request it must be aware that it depends upon them as to whether or not they will be healed.

Regardless of the method used, success is not always factual for the requestee. This is true of all methods of this nature, like Lourdes or Oral Roberts' touch by hand.

BRAD: Can you determine what percentage of your correspondents are cured by your method of healing?

TWITCHELL: I cannot give you a percentage of success in this field, mainly because so many people do not know how to communicate. They merely write saying that they feel better. Usually, in doing so, they tend to project their feelings into other requests for themselves.

This is discouraging, for it seems to indicate that they consider their bodies like a machine that can be easily repaired. By the same token, if they regard themselves like, for example, an automobile, that is all the more reason why they should give the healer an accurate report of themselves. When parts start to go on an old car, something else is bound to go very soon. The healer should know that the right source was not healed.

BRAD: Can someone request healing for a third party?

TWITCHELL: No one should ask for healing except for himself, otherwise he may be interfering with the freedom of someone else's state of consciousness.

For example, some people do not want to be healed, for having an affliction gives them certain advantages. They are able to use their affliction as a social lever on others, and since I cannot nor will not have anything to do with controlling others and their social conduct, it is a waste of time to ask this.

Once a mother asked me to 'heal' her son of drinking. My reply to her was to let him ask for himself. Perhaps he liked to drink. Perhaps he did not want to change. Therefore, this was not my problem and would not be until the son himself would make it my problem by his own request.

BRAD: How do you accomplish absentee healing?

TWITCHELL: Frankly, I, of myself, do not heal, but it is the Spirit flowing through me, using me as a channel. If I am in a high or total state of consciousness, I am able to work with anyone who wants healing. But again, I cannot guarantee success. This is because, *first*, Spirit makes its own choice of whether it will heal anyone; its innate wisdom knows better than anyone in the human state of consciousness what is best for anyone personally.

Second, if one must finish out a piece of karma (the divine laws of debt and credit, cause and effect) then Spirit will not interfere whatsoever. I have had to tell people, who have been disappointed because of a lack of healing, that I neither outline nor direct Spirit what to do. I can only request it to heal a person.

I once made a request of this spiritual power to give a man a job opportunity, as he had requested, but instead, the man got a healing. Spirit knew that this man needed a health problem handled before he could work effectively. The man was dissatisfied at first, but later he found excellent employment.

Another point to be made here is that Spirit flowing through myself will dissolve the problems of another within the Cosmic Consciousness. While this is true, I must be careful not to take on the karmic problem of anyone who has made the request of myself.

This has happened a few times, and when I discovered what had happened, I turned it over to Spirit, which took care of the problem. Neither will I touch anyone who has a karmic debt to be paid, except maybe to help lighten the load. Otherwise, I am interfering with spiritual law.

BRAD: Is it, then, a spiritual force which accomplishes the actual healing?

TWITCHELL: Yes, it is Spirit that flows through the channel, lifting up the human state of consciousness, correcting all errors in it. But one must distinguish between the psychic and the spiritual states.

There are healings via the psychic, or mental, state of consciousness, but these healings are not likely to stay. It is an unstable force, a lower force than that of the spiritual, and even though certain healings have been accomplished with mental force, it is not likely that the cure will be permanent.

BRAD: Should one always heal? Are there times when you might refuse to heal someone because of certain factors of which you, in your heightened state of perception, may be aware?

TWITCHELL: One must always consider the survival factor of the individual who is to be healed. If the person has a good survival attitude, by that I mean that he has hope, faith, a cheerful disposition and a strong desire to achieve positive results, he is more likely to have good, permanent healing.

But those persons who are in non-survival states wallow in grief, misery, lack of faith, apathy. Such attitudes are not likely to bring about healing.

For example, one woman wrote, 'I would like to have you try to heal me, but I have tried four other healers. I doubt if you can help me, but you may try if you wish.'

This woman prided herself on her lack of faith toward healers, but yet she hoped that a miracle might happen. I promptly forgot her. She was in the non-survival area.

BRAD: Speaking of miracles, do they occur in absentee healing?

TWITCHELL: Timing on any healing depends on certain factors, too. There are miracles, spontaneous healings, which happen at once. There are also healings which take time. Occasionally I will give a time limit on a healing, such as ten days, and the requestee will write back to inform me that the healing has been accomplished within the time limit which I have set.

It is enjoyable to be able to help people in this manner. Many people begin to receive their healing as soon as they drop their letters to me in the mail box. Spirit knows and will start working for them, as I am only a channel for Spirit to flow through, to touch all things and lift them up, through healing, better living conditions, and the repairing of human relationships. Most of all, I seek to give them greater love for all things—especially life and God.

Spiritual Travelers and Golden Temples

One brisk, autumn night in 1967, Paul Twitchell, the living ECK master, and I walked the streets of Chicago until after midnight.

We had so much more freedom in those days. Paul had no major conferences then, only small gatherings of the faithful. There were not yet the hundreds of thousands of chelas surrounding their Master for a smile, a handshake, a touch on the shoulder. Destiny would soon decree that things would be changing very soon. Paul's life would be a whirlwind until his sudden transition in 1971.

Paul laughed and suggested that we had been walking along State Street for so long that we might soon be considered suspicious characters. His blue eyes always crinkled at the corners when he was amused.

I agreed, but told him how much I enjoyed sharing our thoughts with one another. In another time, we might have been talking and walking all night through the streets of ancient Rome or Greece, beneath the shadow of a pyramid, on a dusty road through the streets of Jerusalem.

"Or on a snowy trail in the mountainous regions of Tibet," Paul continued, catching the spirit of my analogy. "And you know, Brad, maybe we did just that. Maybe we've walked through the night and talked like this in many previous incarnations."

We returned to the hotel and talked even later into the night about Soul Travel, as Paul termed it; out-of-body-experiences or astral projection, as I called it.

I explained my elementary technique of focusing on a candle flame, placing myself in light trance, then giving energy to the thought that I would leave my body.

Paul asked me if I had encountered any of the entities that he termed Spiritual Travelers, the "fierce Godmen of Light," such as Rebazar Tarzs, Gopal Das, and others. In Eckankar, these Masters allegedly help students gather inner experiences and teach them how to describe them, according to their examples.

I told Paul about the beautiful multi-dimensional golden temple wherein I had received instructions since earliest childhood. I had a profound recollection of the monk-like appearance of the teacher's physical body; but, for some reason, I could not distinguish his face.

Paul advised me to continue to heed those dream teachings. He assured me that the Masters would provide me with instructional materials, just as they had always done.

What Paul Twitchell defined as Soul Travel was the movement of the Soul in the lower worlds, that of the regions from the physical planes to the fifth plane, "which is the first of those ethereal regions named as the world of pure spirit." In the lower worlds, according to Paul, we are concerned with travel and movement. "But when we reach the upper planes of God, there is no time and space concept. Travel is not needed, and we are in the state of total awareness—that is, God Realization, or absolute consciousness."

Paul felt that anyone could do Soul Travel, whether under the direction of a spiritual teacher or not. But he felt it made good sense to have a teacher, a guru, in the beginning.

"There is no genuine, no true and sincere master who would seek to hold his chela forever," Paul told me. "The real master will always release his student after that student has established himself or herself on the fifth plane of consciousness. Once students have achieved this stage, their feet are firmly planted on the illuminated path of God."

In Twitchell's cosmology, the basic principle of Soul Travel is that we are truly spirit-selves and that we can take charge of our subtle bodies and can move from the visible planes into the invisible worlds at will.

An Out-Of-Body Technique

Twitchell often shared the following technique for achieving an elementary out-of-body projection on the lower planes:

Just before going to bed at night, you should sit in an easy chair or on the floor, back erect, and concentrate your attention on the spiritual eye between the eyebrows. Chanting "Aum," or some other comfortable mantra, during this period of concentration is recommended.

While focusing on the spiritual eye and chanting, Paul suggested that you hold your attention on a black screen in the inner vision, doing your best to keep that screen free from any mental pictures.

In order to prevent unwanted mental images from flashing

upward, Paul suggested the placing of an image of Christ, a saint, or some holy figure of personal importance in their place.

After a few minutes, there suddenly may come a faint clicking sound in one ear, or a sound similar to that of a cork popping. You then will find yourself outside the body, looking back at the physical shell sitting in the easy chair on the floor. At this point, the Essential Self, the real person is ready for a short journey in the other worlds.

Paul stressed that there is nothing to fear when you are out of the body. No harm can come to the mind traveler. Nor can any harm come to the physical body when it is left behind.

Although you may not always be aware of the presence, Paul stated, a teacher or guru will be standing by to keep watch over the student's progress. Then, after a short journey through Time and Space, the spirit body will return and slide gently in the physical body with a light jolt.

A Sense of Oneness with All

Paul Twitchell and I talked most of that fall night in Chicago. Then, after we had exchanged our wishes for a restful sleep, I excused myself to go to my own room.

I yawned most of the way down the hallway. It had been an extremely full day. I had caught an early morning flight, done two radio shows and one television appearance before I met Paul at O'Hare Airport. We had dinner, walked over half of downtown Chicago, and talked until the wee hours. Standard Operating Procedure for the two of us.

I entered my room, wearily fell across the bed, not even bothering to turn on the light. I had dropped my hat on the dresser, but I still held my coat folded over my arms. I lay on my back, just staring at the ceiling.

A tapping sound at the window drew my attention to the glass panes. It had begun to rain, and the wind was driving the drops heavily against the window. The Chicago skyline blurred and ran into watery swirls.

I felt totally relaxed, tranquil, at peace.

Certain of Paul's words came back to me, and a warm glow came over me. It was good to be able to discuss such heavy spiritual and philosophical matters with one who had devoted his entire life to acquiring such knowledge and wisdom.

I felt a marvelous sense of Oneness with the All.

Suddenly, it was as though I was becoming an observer to the innocuous scene of a weary man lying across his hotel bed. It seemed as though I were watching the mundane tableau in some theater of the obscure. I cannot say that I had any sense of seeing myself on the bed, but I was next overcome by a wondrous vibration of total freedom.

Then I was rushing toward the ceiling.

I had a vague impression that I would be mashed against the plaster, that I could not negotiate solid against solid. But a greater Knowing told me that I was no longer solid, no longer dense mass. The molecules of the plaster, steel and brick tickled me as I passed through them. The normally solid matter seemed to be composed of air bubbles.

There was no time, but in what would have been the next few seconds, I was rushing through the rain, soaring above the Chicago streets. I experienced a very slight coolness and heard a sound like that of wind rushing through forest trees.

There was no space, but in the next twinkling instant I was at the Marshall Field Museum of Natural History, Soldiers Field, the Lincoln Park Zoo.

I had only to think of a Chicago landmark, and I was there. Instantly.

I thought of the God Realms, and brilliant explosions of light erupted around me. Incredible lovely purples, golds, blues, greens, and oranges appeared in vibrant hues.

There were quick flashes of a lush garden, a richly productive orchard, a silver stream, a beautiful golden temple. A cowled, monk-like figure stood on the nine golden steps which led upward to a massive golden door.

I reached out my hand, but he kept his arms folded across his broad chest. I could not see his face under the cowl.

Then an elastic band seemed to be pulling me back. Frustrated, angry, I tried to fight against its relentless tugging. A purple mist foamed up around me.

And I was on my back, lying across the hotel bed, my coat still folded in my arms. The wind-borne rain was pelting the window, making the neon lights of the city run together in vertical puddles down toward the panes.

I shook my head slowly in wonder, hastily undressed, and draped my clothing over the nearest chair. I fell into a deep sleep the moment my head touched the pillow.

16

The Beam of a "Mental Flashlight"

A compassionate desire to aid a fellow human in pain inspired the hypnotist Loring G. Williams to fashion the construct of the healing beam of a "mental flashlight." In numerous experiments, the hypnotist instructed entranced mind travellers to "see" individuals in x-ray form and to diagnose their ailments and diseases.

In many cases these diagnoses were passed along to orthodox medical doctors who could use the information as they chose. Some doctors acknowledged that the diagnoses acquired through mind travel complemented their own evaluations of patients' maladies; others did not respond in any manner, negatively or positively.

"Bill" Williams noticed that the mind travellers seemed always to see the illness, bone damage, or nervous condition as a "black spot" within the target individual's body.

My friend Rita was serving as subject, and we were "looking in" on another friend of mine in England. Bill suggested that Rita train a bright "flashlight beam" on the dark areas and dissolve them with light. Rita's reaction was to squint her closed eyes, furrow her forehead, and visibly apply great concentration on areas that remained unseen to our eyes. She sighed, and then said, "Okay. They're gone."

Had the illness really been erased? My friend was in England, too far away to respond quickly. But another friend of mine who was extremely skeptical about spontaneous healing was close by. With a broad grin on his face, he asked Rita if she might "burn away" a small cyst on his ankle.

He had mentioned it to me before the session began that evening, and explained that, although it had been adjudged benign by his family physician, it had appeared virtually overnight. His doctor recommended that it be removed by simple surgery. Later that night, after Rita had focused her "beam" on him, he told me "I actually felt heat in my ankle, and when I lifted the leg of my trousers, the lump had disappeared."

In order to test the most unusual "mental flashlight" a bit further, I put in a call to Dr. J., our family physician, the next day and asked him to select, at random, a number of cases from his files and bring them to my office that afternoon. I explained briefly what we were attempting to achieve, and although he was dubious of any results we might attain, he was not skeptical about hypnosis. One of his instructors in medical school had accomplished a difficult leg amputation while the patient rested peacefully in a state of hypnoanesthesia.

Dr. J. generously devoted a portion of his golfing afternoon that day to assist us with a number of experiments in out-of-body diagnosis. Our *modus operandi* was quite simple. Bill would place Rita in a trance and direct her mentally to a patient whose name and address were supplied by Dr. J. When she felt she was in the presence of the target personality, Rita would describe the patient's physical appearance for verification by Dr. J.

Once Dr. J. acknowledged that she was accurate, Rita would "see" the patient in x-ray form and describe the particular physical malfunctions as she perceived them in the hypnotic state.

Dr. J. was favorably impressed by Rita's ability to describe accurately the target patient's physical appearance, but he was dismayed by the vague general manner in which Rita described the various ailments. In fact, such terms as "abdominal area" can mean something quite different to a layperson than they do to a trained anatomist and physician.

Although Dr. J. conceded that Rita did hit on some of the ailments with a degree of accuracy, some of the other descriptions were obscured by her lack of knowledge of basic anatomy and her meager medical vocabulary.

"But wouldn't this all be interesting if you hypnotized a trained medical student to do this sort of thing?" Dr. J. speculated.

Rita could apparently "see" blighted areas within the patient's body, but her ability to describe them and to diagnose them would be considered most rudimentary to a highly trained diagnostician such as Dr. J. However, Rita's inability to name the affected portions of the body did nothing to negate her incredible ability to "shine the light" on them and to implement healing.

I believe such-out-of-body diagnosis should only be used as an aid, or complement, to orthodox medical practice. Healing is more an art that it is a science, and the same treatment may not always work in the same way for every patient. There are so many variables and subtle mental factors involved in healing. The delicate relationship between doctor and patient, the patient's will to recover, the doctor's own confidence in his or her ability to heal—all remain intangibles forever out of reach of test tube, mortar and pestle.

That out-of-body diagnosis and out-of-body therapy should supplant the physician is the last thing I would suggest. Rather, I challenge the medical establishment to investigate hypnotically controlled out-of-body diagnosis without bias.

Consider the case of G. W.'s feet.

G. W. and his wife sat in on our experiments solely as observers and witnesses. On the particular night they attended, Rita was going about the circle of witnesses "reading" their past and present health conditions. When she got to G. W., she at once picked up an old high school football injury and a more recent injury to his feet.

Some individuals requested that Rita "shine her light" on them that night so they might assess the results for themselves. After Rita had described the damage done to G. W.'s feet, his wife suggested that she attempt to "erase" the great areas of darkness which she perceived in that area.

I shook my head before Bill reinforced Rita's hypnotic suggestion.

"Don't bother," I whispered to Williams.

"Why not?" Williams frowned.

"There's no use," I told him. "G. W. is scheduled for amputation in three months."

I had known G. W. for about a year and had become familiar with the painful history of his terribly damaged feet. G. W. had fallen out of a helicopter when he was in the military service and both feet had been thoroughly smashed.

Physicians had tried every form of therapy and repair throughout the course of ten years; the last resort—amputation—was now all that remained for G. W. He had already resigned himself to six months in a wheelchair and the awkward process of learning to walk all over again.

Williams merely shrugged. "Never too late," he said.

"It is in this case," I insisted. "The medics are going to shave off his toes in October. It has gone past the treatment stage. They've already set a date for the amputation."

"Then he has nothing to lose, has he?" Williams pointed out. I could hardly argue with his logic, and I stepped back so that Williams might again direct Rita to shine her extraordinary mental light over the dark spots on G. W.'s feet.

A month later an excited G. W. telephoned me to say that his scheduled amputation had been called off. Pleased, but puzzled, doctors were talking in hushed tones about a "medical miracle." They were at a loss to explain how the alleged miracle had come to pass.

Some time later, G. W. called with two exciting developments in his case: (1) A correspondent from a medical journal arrived to take pictures of his feet for an article on the strange and sudden healing process which had taken place; (2) While walking in Chicago, his long insensate feet had developed blisters. He was rejoicing because he could once again feel his feet.

17

Astral Healing with the Love Force

I believe that the "gifts" of prophecy, healing, telepathy, and so forth, can be developed much sooner if you utilize altered-states-of-consciousness (ASC). I also believe that the ability to practice astral projection (Soul Travel, out-of-body experience) is extremely important as a tool to fashioning more complete skills of the psyche. I feel that this ability of the human psyche opens the doorways to all other facets of the spirit. Once you have learned to project your spirit from its temple of flesh, all other things will be opened to you.

I am now going to present a meditation that can place you into a relaxed physical state wherein you can accomplish healing through astral travel. Be optimistic and positive. By the same token, expect that it may take you more that one session to become an expert mind traveler.

Since this technique deals with color and repetitious progressions, it is quite easy to memorize and use in placing yourself in an altered state. Or, you may wish to record a cassette of your voice ahead of time and thereby be your own guide through the experience. If you have like-minded friend or family member to guide you, so much the better.

You will find it extremely helpful to play a recording of music that suggests a mood of "lifting" away. Any music that is swelling, inspirational, will do. Just be certain that it is instrumental only, for lyrics will distract you by suggesting other images than the ones desired. I recommend the works of Steven Halpern or Iasos for meditation and for achieving altered states.

Technique for Connecting with the Love Force

Sit in a chair, lie on your bed, lean against a wall—whatever position is most comfortable for you. Select a time when you will not be disturbed. Disconnect the telephone. Turn on your music.

Visualize that at your feet lies a rose-colored blanket. The color rose stimulates natural body warmth and induces sleep. It also provides you with a sense of well-being and a great feeling of being loved.

Now you see that the blanket is really a kind of auric cover, a rose-colored auric cover. Imagine that you are *willing* the blanket-like aura to move slowly up your body.

Feel it moving over your feet, relaxing them; over your legs, relaxing them; over your stomach, easing all tensions; moving over your chest, your arms, your neck.

Now, as you make a hood of the rose-colored auric cover, imagine that the color of rose permeates your psyche and does its part in activating your ability to project love and healing energy to others. Once you have done this, visualize yourself bringing the rose-colored aura over your head.

The color green serves as a disinfectant, a cleanser. It also influences the proper building of muscle and tissue.

Imagine that you are pulling a green, blanket-like aura over your body. Feel it moving over your feet, cleansing them; feel it moving over your legs, healing them of all pains. Feel it moving over your stomach, ridding it of all pains. Feel it moving over your chest, your arms, your neck—cleansing them, healing them.

As you make a hood of the green-colored auric cover, imagine that the color of green permeates your psyche and does its part in activating your ability to use the love energy to cleanse and to strengthen others. Once you have done this, visualize yourself bringing the green colored aura over your head.

Gold strengthens the nervous system and helps you become calm. It also aids digestion.

Visualize now that you are pulling a soft, beautiful golden aura slowly over your body. Feel it moving over your feet, calming you. Feel it moving over your legs, relaxing them. Feel it moving over your stomach, soothing any nervous condition. Feel it moving over your chest, your arms, your neck.

As you make a comfortable hood of the golden aura, imagine that the color of gold permeates your psyche and strengthens your nervous system so that your body-brain network will serve as a better conduit for the forces of healing and love. Once you have done this, visualize yourself bringing the gold-colored aura over your head. Once you have done this, visualize yourself bringing the gold-colored aura over your head.

Researchers have discovered that red-orange strengthens and cleanses the lungs. In our modern society with its pollution problems, our lungs become fouled whether or not we smoke cigarettes. Yogis and other masters have long known that effective meditation, effective ASC, can be achieved best through proper techniques of breathing through clean lungs.

Therefore, visualize before you a red-orange cloud of pure oxygen. Take a comfortably deep breath and visualize some of that red-orange cloud moving into your lungs. Imagine it traveling through your lungs, cleansing them, purifying them, bearing away particles of impurities.

Now, visualize yourself *exhaling* that red-orange cloud from your lungs. See how spoiled and darkly-colored it is with impurities.

Take another comfortably deep breath. Again, see the red-orange cloud of pure, clean oxygen moving into your lungs. See the red-orange cloud purifying your lungs of the negative effects of exhaust fumes, smoke, industrial gases.

Exhale the impurities, then breathe again of the purifying, cleansing red-orange cloud.

Yellow-orange will help oxygen move into every organ and gland of your body, purifying them, cleansing them.

Imagine before you now a yellow-orange cloud of pure oxygen. Take a comfortably deep breath and inhale that cleansing, purifying yellow-orange cloud into your lungs. Feel the yellow-orange cloud moving through your body. Feel it cleansing and purifying every organ. Feel it cleansing and purifying every gland. If you have any area of weakness or disease anywhere in your body, feel the yellow-orange energy bathing it in cleansing, healing vibrations.

As you exhale all impurities and inhale again the pure, clean, yellow-orange cloud of oxygen, visualize the healing process taking place throughout your body. As you exhale and inhale, see your body becoming pure and clean. See now that the cloud you exhale is as clean and pure as that which is being inhaled. You have cleared and purified your lungs. You have cleansed, purified, and healed all of your body and all its organs.

Blue is the color of psychic ability. This color increases visionary potential.

Visualize a blue, blanket-like aura beginning to move over your body. Feel it moving over your feet, relaxing them. Feel it moving over your legs, soothing them. Feel it moving over your stomach, your chest, your arms, your neck, soothing them, relaxing them.

As you make a hood of the blue-colored auric cover, imagine that the color blue permeates your psyche and does its part in activating your ability to use the God Force to transmit love and healing. Once you have done this, visualize yourself bringing the blue-colored aura over your head.

The color violet serves as an excellent muscle relaxant. Violet is a tranquilizer. It is the color of the highest vibration.

Imagine that you are pulling a violet, blanket-like aura over your body. Feel it moving over your feet, relaxing them. Feel it moving over your legs, relaxing them, soothing them. Feel it moving over your stomach, removing all tensions. Feel it moving over your chest, your arms, your neck, tranquilizing them, relaxing them.

Now, as you fashion a hood of the violet-colored auric cover, imagine that the color of violet permeates your psyche and does its part in activating your ability to use the God Energy for healing. Feel the color violet attuning your psyche to the highest vibration. Feel the color violet connecting your psyche to the God-energy. Once you have done this, visualize yourself bringing the violet-colored aura over your head.

You are now lying or sitting, totally wrapped in your violet-colored auric cover. You are very secure, very comfortable, very relaxed. Your mind is very receptive, very aware. You feel attuned with a Higher Consciousness. You feel as though your awareness has been expanded. You feel prepared to explore deep, deep within yourself, deep within (For the next portion of this exercise, I recommend "Tarashanti" by Georgia Kelley, or any recording of restful flute music.)

You are seeing memory patterns before you. They may be your memories of a past-life experience, or the memories of another person. It does not matter. You are seeing them form before you now. The memories are taking you to a faraway place, a faraway time, on the vibration of the Eternal Now. You see a blue, blue sky...mountains...a large city made of stone, high in the mountains. You are remembering an ancient city hidden in the mountains.

You remember that you were a student there, a very special student of a very special teacher—a healer, a master, who served only good.

This great healer has made you his or her prize pupil. You, more than any of the other initiates, have responded perfectly to the sound of the healer's wondrous flute. When the master-teacher blows this flute, you are able to leave your body. When the master-healer blows the flute, you soar free of your physical limitations. You soar high above the mountains. You soar free of Time and Space. You can go anywhere you wish, instantly. You have but to think it and you are there...to heal, to ease the pains and sorrows of others.

You are proud that you have become your master's special student. You are proud that of all the students in this great city of love and light, you are the one who has been selected for the great demonstration.

Now you are walking through the streets of the city, surrounded by the other students. It is night. There is a full Moon. You are walking to a place in the mountains where you will give the demonstration.

Look around you. Remember the faces of those nearest you. Remember the faces of those standing in the streets watching you. Remember the houses, the city walls.

Now you are approaching the area of the demonstration. It is a grassy place ringed by great rocks. You see that your mater-teacher, the great healer, is already there. Your teacher stands on one of the highest rocks, robe blowing gently in the mountain breeze, flute in hand.

Twelve students step forward from the crowd and form a circle around a blanket that has been spread on the grass. You step into the circle, advance to the blanket. You take a deep breath and lie down on the blanket.

You look up at the full Moon. A small cloud moves across its face. You lie quietly for a few moments, then raise your arm to signal that you are ready.

You lie on the blanket, on your back, looking up at the full Moon. You are calm. You are relaxed. You know that when you hear the sound of the flute, you will soar free of your body. You essential self, the Real You that exists within, will burst free of the limitations of the physical body and shoot up toward the sky, toward the Moon.

The Great Healer, your master-teacher, lifts the flute...and blows...

You feel yourself rushing, pushing, pulsating, spinning...bursting free of your body!

You, the Real You, soar toward the Moon.

Down below, you can see the students and your master-teacher. But your Universe is only you and the sound of the healing flute.

Go with the sound. Go wherever you wish. You have but to think it and you will be there...instantly.

Think of a loved one...a loved one who is faraway. You have but to think of that loved one and you will be there...instantly. You are beside that loved one instantly, to transmit love and healing.

The sound takes you there. The sound of the flute takes you there. Go with the sound. Go wherever you wish...wherever you are needed.

Practice this technique every *other* night for as long as it takes you to accomplish a successful astral projection. You may continue to use the color meditation to place yourself in a deep, altered state. Once you have traveled successfully to a few target areas, you own creative principle will begin to suggest variations on the exercise to you.

Whether an OBE is but an imaginative manner in which to express traveling clairvoyance is a question some parapsychologists enjoy debating. Such a matter need not concern us as healers. We are pragmatists, and our primary interest is the results we attain.

18

The Magic of Body-Mind Control

Manipulation of the physical body, as well the mind and spirit, can bring about good health and accelerate the healing process. In this chapter, we shall emphasize the Oneness of the mind-body-spirit trinity.

The Masseur Who Saved 60,000 Lives

"Somehow," the Nazi officer snarled in a half-joking, half-serious tone, "I must break you of your one outrageous flaw. How can you love those accursed Jews?"

The masseur smiled, but allowed none of his true feelings to show in his face. Instead, he kneaded the Nazi's back more gently. "Perhaps because I see them as a part of the human race."

"Hah! You should listen more closely to your Fuhrer."

"Roll over please," the masseur directed.

The man on the padded table turned obediently, revealing the face of Heinrich Himmler, second officer of the German Reich, to the light. "I could have you shot, tortured, dismembered..."

The masseur nodded. But he knew Himmler would not, and Himmler knew he knew it.

"Ach," Himmler snorted in disgust. "How many of the dogs must we release this time?"

"Five hundred," the masseur said evenly, the lips in his smooth face barely moving as he spoke.

For a moment sparks seemed to fly from the Nazi's eyes, then he relaxed and the massage continued. A few moments later the high-ranking Nazi reached over the table and pushed a button.

"He wants five hundred this time," he said aloud into a microphone built into the wall.

"Five hundred, sir?"

"You heard me," Himmler snapped.

"Yes, sir."

"Kersten," Himmler said testily, "you are the most abominable necessity I've ever had."

To that, the masseur smiled.

Felix Kersten, born in Finland, had studied agriculture until joining the army of Finland during World War I. Although the art of massage had become very sophisticated in Finland, Kersten had had no inclination to study it until after the war, when he was convalescing in a Helsinki hospital. Contemplating the future, the opportunities seemed very limited.

Although he had been trained in agriculture, Kersten no longer had any land to work. His army career had ended abruptly with his wound. Besides, he did not desire to follow the military life.

Every day he associated with men he admired—the doctors who cared for him. Kersten resolved to join their ranks, but when he confided in a doctor about his new-found ambition, the medic discouraged him.

The doctor patiently explained that years of schooling would be necessary and would not be easy for a man with no preliminary training or funds. The doctor then suggested that the young Kersten begin a study of massage.

"Your hands are ideally suited for it," the doctor explained, looking at Kersten's short fingers.

The doctor convinced the young officer to at least talk to the masseurs on the hospital staff before dismissing the notion of massage altogether. With his first attempts, Kersten found that he had a gift for the art, and the hospital staff was astounded at this great talent. He became the favorite masseur for all the soldiers who came to the Helsinki hospital. Felix Kersten knew great joy when he discovered he could bring health and comfort to men's bodies with his hands.

Kersten came under the tutelage of a well-known specialist named Dr. Killandar. This man had great success in treating patients, and Kersten soon became his devoted pupil. Although he never missed a lecture, class, or demonstration, Kersten worked part-time to earn enough money to eat while he studied. In 1921, he received a degree in scientific massage, and Dr. Killandar told his prize pupil that he would have to journey to Germany to further his studies.

Once again the masseur paid his rent and filled his stomach by working odd jobs in Berlin. Although never able to live an affluent life, Kersten kept his good spirits by patient devotion to his work.

He studied under a famous surgeon and teacher, Professor Bier. This well-known man, though accepted as an authority in every corner of the world, had idiosyncrasies which often disturbed his more orthodox colleagues. He investigated the more unconventional forms of healing, and his open-minded devotion to the single goal of alleviating suffering often brought him criticism in the drawing rooms of Berlin.

Through Bier, Kersten met a Tibetan monk named Dr. Ko. The small, elderly, wrinkled man had come from the Orient to complete his study of the masseur's art.

Kersten first accepted the monk only because Bier had introduced them, but he later found that the wrinkled old man, whose face wore a perpetual smile, knew approaches and techniques which no Western masseur had ever thought of trying. Where Kersten had thought himself quite accomplished, Dr. Ko quickly convinced him that he knew very little.

Backed by centuries of study and tradition, Dr. Ko introduced Kersten to Oriental massage, and the Finn had not studied the monk's techniques for very long before he realized just how primitive Western methods were. Oriental massage incorporated facets of Yoga and Oriental philosophy in which the masseur himself built a bond of great empathy between himself and his patient.

Most important to the treatment of pain was the diagnosis of cause, and most important to the diagnosis were the sensitive fingertips of the masseur.

To be a successful masseur, the pupil had to devote his entire being to the art, and that Kersten did with great zeal. He admired the little monk, not only as a practitioner, but also as a man. Dr. Ko had great fortitude, courage and endurance, and he cheerfully accepted all that life offered with the smile that forever graced his face.

Thus, Kersten seemed set adrift when the little man bade him goodbye and returned to his Tibetan monastery. For a time Kersten felt himself torn between the Orient and the Occident, but as time passed, he made peace within himself and began to apply his long education.

Word of his great talent spread throughout Europe. Perhaps his most famous pre-World War II patient was the Prince Consort, husband of Queen Wilhelmina of the Netherlands. The man suffered from severe stomach pains which only Kersten could relieve.

During the war, Kersten found himself a virtual prisoner of Heinrich Himmler, who suffered from the same stomach disorder as the Prince Consort. Himmler became completely dependent on the masseur's soothing fingers, and Kersten used his position to great advantage.

Not only did Kersten receive official exoneration from a charge of collaborating with the Nazis, but the Netherlands made him a Grand Officer of the Orange Nassau for his personal intervention which saved many Dutch lives and much Dutch treasure from the Nazis. The World Jewish Congress credits the Finn with the rescue of sixty thousand Jews doomed to certain death by Himmler. Felix Kersten died a very respected man in 1960.

"It is the very essence of love, of nobleness, of greatness, to be willing to suffer for the good of others."

Rev. I. Smith Spencer

Emile Coue: Master of the Mind Cure

In the last years of the nineteenth century, French doctors and psychologists became enthusiastic about experiments in healing through hypnotism. These pioneers in psychosomatic medicine were deluded into believing hypnotism could heal every disease.

"The patient need only to be hypnotized into a state of vibrant health," assured one Gallic practitioner, speaking to his colleagues at a medical convention in 1892 in Paris. "The promise of hypnotism will eventually empty the hospitals and mental institutions."

Despite such glowing testimonials from these early experimenters, it was soon discovered that not every patient could be hypnotized. Even more confusing, some patients did not accept hypnotic suggestions as a permanent part of their personalities.

These early psychologists were unable to answer the question of how any patient, even a diagnosed hysteric, could become susceptible to a variety of physical diseases. "And how does hypnotism cure some, but not all?" asked a puzzled psychologist.

Today, hypnotic therapy has shown vividly how the power of the mind can influence our bodies. One of the most important schools of curing through suggestibility was established by a pudgy, confident French druggist named Emile Coue.

After reading about experiments in hypnotism, Coue asked, "Is the hypnotist really necessary? Is it possible for the patient, or the individual, to make his own suggestions to his subconscious mind?"

As he filled prescriptions in his quaint French drugstore,

Emile Coue experimented with the healing powers of the mind. After many years, he announced his hypothesis:

"The key is to repeat your suggestions when the mind is most receptive to messages," said Coue. "This occurs immediately after you have awakened from a deep sleep or just prior to falling asleep."

Coue's method seemed to work. His success skyrocketed and more than a hundred patients a day crowded into his small drug shop. "Every morning and evening you must repeat, 'Every day in every way I am getting better and better.' Don't think about the meaning of those words. You're just telegraphing the message to your subconscious mind."

Actually, Emile Coue had stumbled onto an astounding psychiatric discovery. "When the will and imagination are battling, imagination will always win," he emphasized.

As an example, Coue cited the rheumatic patient who determinedly says, "I will move my body without any pain." If the sufferer's mind is filled with doubt, it becomes impossible to move without pain.

"The phrase 'I can' is the release," said Coue. "Our imagination, not our will power, transmits an idea into the subconscious mind. Once an idea has been placed in the subconscious, anything is possible because the subconscious rules the body." Coue cited hypnotism as ample proof of this theory.

Coue's amazing cures read like something out of the wildest claims of a glib, fast-talking faith healer.

A physician brought a teen-aged tubercular girl to the French druggist. "I have done everything possible to save her life," said the physician. "It may help to try your suggestibility treatments."

The cheerful druggist discovered that the doomed girl was highly receptive to suggestion. "After three months, I examined the patient and there was not a spot of tuberculosis," said the grateful physician.

Coue's healing suggestions cured virtually every type of illness and his "I can" incantations swept the world. Schools were established. Books and magazines were printed on the art of suggestibility. Some practitioners tried to cure not only illness, but to change personalities and bring limitless wealth and personal happiness. "Anyone can have anything through auto-suggestion," became a slogan of the "Roaring Twenties."

Just as with its psychological predecessors in France, Coueism was soon shown to have definite limitations. Perhaps some people were unable to believe and self-doubt clouded their minds. Some were unconvinced of the power of suggestibility. Many scientists scoffed openly at the supposed cures produced by Coueism. After the fad faded in America, a national magazine "exposed" the method by revealing that many supposedly miraculous healings had been only temporary.

Nevertheless, the repetitive "Every day in every way I am getting better and better" did produce some remarkable cures for many people. Just as faith healing seldom works for an atheist, Coueism failed for those without sufficient belief.

Emile Coue was not a healer who appeared on the scene and then disappeared. Although he died in 1926, his books were reprinted in 1961. A small cluster of followers continues to spread the remarkable news of auto-suggestion through the world today.

The Gentle Mind Healer

Phineas Parkhurst Quimby wanted everybody to understand how the mind could influence the body. A simple man, Quimby had a penetrating mind and a keen natural intellect, which kept him forever searching for ways to help alleviate suffering and disease.

Although he began his adult life as a clock maker and an inventor, he had always nurtured a deep interest in people. Quimby did not possess an extensive formal education, but he read voraciously, especially philosophy and science. His reading led him away from established religions and creeds, even though he espoused the truths that Jesus of Nazareth taught through the New Testament.

Quimby made no sudden conversion from clock making

to mental healer but, rather, came to his conclusions slowly, his opinions evolving over periods of time after much deliberation. If any single incident could be called a turning point in his life, it would be his attendance at a demonstration given by a hypnotist named Charles Poyen. Quimby developed such an interest in hypnotism that he followed Poyen to several towns, until at last, he began trying hypnotism himself.

Later, Quimby observed John B. Dodd and a teenager, Lucius Burmar, making a tour of New England. The pair employed clairvoyance to diagnose illness and to prescribe drugs which could be used as a cure. With young Burmar as a medium, Quimby was able to get the same results as Dodd, even though he prescribed simpler, less expensive drugs.

Quimby then came to the conclusion that the drugs themselves had little effect on a patient. It was, he decided, the patient's faith in the cure that did the healing. Quimby began investigating this notion until he found that suggestion alone was powerful enough to cure. He dispensed with the drugs and the teenager altogether.

Quimby's method consisted of gaining great empathy and kinship with the patient while allowing the patient to gain complete confidence in him. This he did by conversation. He rarely accepted money, but demanded—indeed, needed—the complete faith of the patient.

In some cases Quimby would place his hands upon an ill person, but he claimed that this only focused the patient's attention on the healing and was most effective when the patient believed that such touches would heal.

Quimby took no credit for the healing at all. He claimed that he acted like a lens which focused the healing power of the patient's mind onto the illness or pain. Quimby's extensive record of successful healings is even more remarkable when it is remembered that most of his patients had tried nearly every other cure, and that more orthodox healers had given them no comfort.

Quimby's most famous patient was a woman named Mrs. Patterson of Portland, Maine. Mrs. Patterson is known to the world as Mary Baker Eddy. In 1862, she came to Quimby after years of suffering with cataleptic fits and unexplainable pain. His immediate cure of her maladies had a profound effect on her thought in founding of the Christian Science movement.

Quimby hoped that the woman, who professed to being an authoress, might use her talent with the pen to pass on what he had learned with such patient endeavor. She returned in 1864 and studied with him. Immediately after Quimby's death in 1866, Mary Baker Eddy praised him in print, giving him full credit for his influence on her thought.

Quimby lived a simple life. His neighbors admired and respected him, and he had reputation in the community as an honest, gentle and practical man. He looked on his healing as a method of correcting the errors which humankind itself has made. Since God is good, and so is His creation, Quimby reasoned, *people* must have come by sickness as a result of their own mistakes. Thus, he declared, individuals also could correct their errors through the power of their minds.

On January 16, 1866, Phineas Quimby died of an abdominal tumor which he had kept in check for many years by the force of his will. At last the press of events became too strong, and he succumbed to the spreading growth. Although few people acknowledge him as their leader, Quimby's pioneering work laid the foundation of many schools of thought, including Christian Science, New Thought and Metaphysical Healing.

Evelyn Monahan's Inspirational Journey

In 1961, at the age of twenty-two, Evelyn Monahan began to experience severe mental and physical afflictions resulting from various accidents. One of these accidents had involved a severe blow to the back of her head, causing her to become totally blind. Then, a few months later, she was besieged by epileptic seizures resulting from the same head injury. She was told that the damage to her nervous system was beyond repair and that her afflictions would be permanent.

As if these tragic instances were not enough, she contracted an allergy in 1968 which caused an abscess to form upon her neck. Her doctor, while making an incision to drain the abscess, accidentally severed one of the cranial nerves in her neck. This resulted in permanent paralysis of her right arm and shoulder.

Understandably, Evelyn Monahan became filled with hostility and resentment toward the world. She was blind, partially paralyzed, given to epileptic seizures, and had suffered severe mental and emotional trauma.

Today, however, Evelyn is not blind, nor does she experience epileptic seizures. Today, she enjoys the full use of all her limbs. She directs her own nonprofit research foundation and is a college teacher. She is active in sports, is a published author and lecturer in demand all over the country, and is fast becoming a national luminary in the field of parapsychology.

How was Evelyn Monahan able to overcome such overwhelming physical and emotional handicaps to literally accomplish the "impossible"? She insists that what she refers to as "extended sensory perception" was largely responsible for her return to health.

Evelyn was raised a Catholic and educated in the Catholic school system. After graduating from high school, she spent two years in a cloistered convent.

The spiritual experience still plays a large part in her life, although she has become eclectic in her approach to religion. The reality of a supreme being as she experienced it was a central ingredient in the repair of her physical body. She acknowledges this fact and makes no attempt to apologize for her belief. She decided to employ the positive force of faith and believed she could—and would—be healed, that her faith would "save" her.

The potential of mind over matter was intriguing to the young woman. She and two of her friends evolved an idea through which they hoped Evelyn might be healed. The basic idea was a simple one. The three friends formed a "psychic battery." Their plan was to establish an around-the-clock focus of energy which was to be directed into her body. This healing energy was to take the form of white light which would enter her body and actually change the molecular structure of her brain. The three used a visualization technique wherein they actually "saw" the restoration of the tissues and cells occurring in their minds' eyes.

They catalyzed this process with the application of pure faith that it actually was working at every moment of the treatment. When one person went off the "healing shift," another took it up and continued until she was relieved. Throughout this experiment, Evelyn Monahan had complete faith that God would restore her to good health.

Eventually, her sight returned. Then the epileptic seizures ceased, and control returned to all her physical faculties. The healing technique which restored Evelyn Monahan's sight took a mere five days. The Monahan miracle became fact.

Evelyn Monahan believes this miracle technique is part of a universal principle and can be used by anyone who develops the mental and spiritual muscles to make it work.

Although her physical and mental abilities were impaired for years, Evelyn graduated from college. She received a bachelor's degree in psychology and sociology from the University of Tennessee. She has a master's degree in education from Georgia State and did work in experimental psychology at Emory University. She completed her doctoral studies in educational psychology at Georgia State in Atlanta. Besides this impressive formal education, Evelyn Monahan has been an avid student of parapsychology and psychical research, and is knowledgeable on most aspects of the field.

Evelyn's solid background in science and psychology gives her an edge as a teacher of extended sensory development. She can relate the laws and forces revealed through group experiments so that they make sense to students. She can aid the practical student in recognizing the interaction of energy forces from the physical universe with those invisible forces which may be spiritual or other dimensional.

One significant development has grown out of the publicity and exposure of Evelyn Monahan's techniques. Once, when she was on a radio program, the announcement was made that she was willing to work with the blind in some experiments in extended sensory perception. She made no promises that there would be sensational results, but that she was willing to try. A number of handicapped people responded to her offer.

One young man, who was totally blind, came to her. After his training with Evelyn Monahan, this man has found a very interesting job. He sorts engineering prints—by color! A blind man who sort prints by color has to be an endorsement for extended sensory perception and a major breakthrough in the rehabilitation of the handicapped.

This same young man is also reported to have seen his wedding pictures for the first time. He is still blind, but he can describe what his wife looks like by touching the photographs.

Evelyn Monahan is optimistic that in time these techniques will be perfected to enable the blind will be able to read without braille.

The Whole Body Is a Sensory Mechanism

When asked to speculate about the potential for her techniques of extended sensory perception as they might apply to other forms of disabilities, Evelyn responded: "I have come to believe the whole body is a sensing mechanism. We have been given to accept the role of the five senses performing in a limited, restricted way. The eyes see, the ears hear, the nose smells, the skin feels, the tongue tastes—period. Our experiments indicate that the entire body—every inch of it—is a sensing device.

"Our senses can be extended to feed visual or other information to the brain. The psychic senses are really the extended sensory perceptors of the individual human organism. The deaf, for example, can benefit tremendously from telepathy. We have done research on this and have found that a message received telepathically is received in the language of the receiver, no matter in what language it is sent.

All these techniques for expanding the consciousness will help handicapped people to communicate with us and to understand things better.

"As for understanding psychic abilities in the rest of us, we have a long way to go. I was lucky to have grown up in a family where psychic ability was accepted. I think that a lot of kids get this squashed out of them.

"They may evidence a degree of telepathy, clairvoyance, precognitive dreams, or psychometry as a child. They are told by adults that this cannot be. They are told what their limitations are. Unfortunately, many children accept these explanations and suppress their experiences from then on.

"I think it would be far wiser to teach children their potential (including their psychic abilities) than to concentrate on their limitations. We all have psychic ability, and I believe it can be taught and developed. Naturally, everybody does not have the same amount of psychic talent."

Evelyn Monahan believes in reincarnation. "I may have brought some of these abilities with me into this life. I am quite aware that science is unable to validate reincarnation at this time. I am also aware of genetic and racial memory as explanations for personality and physical characteristics. I take these into consideration, too.

"The idea of reincarnation and karma can really set a person to thinking differently. For instance, the person who believes in reincarnation and thinks he can go out and do anything he wants to since he will get another chance anyway, is totally wrong. It is just the opposite. A person who really believes in reincarnation is going to live a lot more carefully. He is going to try not to hold grudges and do unkind things because he knows he has to resolve this sooner or later.

"One of the things reincarnation did for me was to make it possible for me to mesh the concept of a completely just God with a completely merciful God. I was raised a Catholic, and I could not understand how God could send someone to everlasting damnation—and yet ask me to forgive my enemy seven times seven. Reincarnation gave me the answer. This way God can demand a certain degree of perfection, and give you as many chances as you need to attain this goal.

"To me, life is like living in a car. The body is a vehicle which we use to get around in while we are living this life. Just as an automobile is more than its body, so we are more than just our physical bodies. You can call this spiritual quality the soul, the personality or whatever you wish. I believe it is this part of us which survives after physical death. I have no doubts about this.

"And I do not believe that we go to a place called heaven. Heaven to me is a state of consciousness. So is hell. Hell is a separation from God. I think we create our own hell by separating ourselves from God. It is our nature to be drawn toward God. If we constantly decide not to, we have created our own hell.

"Survival after death is not a question for me. I know there is survival. I look at a table, a book, the great pyramid, and yet I know that one single person is more important than these. I cannot believe that a book or a pyramid can outlast a person."

19

Komar's Program to Conquer Pain

One of my dearest friends is the remarkable Komar (also known as Vernon Craig), who in May of 1986, was among the first five inductees into the *Guinness Book of Records'* Hall of Fame.

Komar holds the world record for such incredible feats of pain control as supporting the heaviest weight (1642-1/2 pounds) while being sandwiched between two beds of nails. This feat is so dangerous, that the Guinness judges have retired the event, thus enabling Komar to retain the record for life. In addition, Komar holds the title of "Human Salamander" for setting a record for the longest and hottest firewalk: twenty-five feet through 1494-degree-fahrenheit bed of coals.

I know this superman as a gentle, loving friend, who has always been there when I needed him. I am also aware that Komar has quietly served as the channel for some truly wonderful healings in his journeys around the world. This smiling apostle of love and light has traveled the globe from China to Tahiti, from Great Britain to Honolulu. And everywhere he goes, he teaches both by word and by his living physical example that pain can be controlled.

By utilizing the various techniques and methods which are outlined in this section, he has been able to keep pain a virtual stranger in life.

"Not long ago," he said, "I received a letter from Thomas B. in Connecticut. Thomas told me that he had been following my step-by-step method to self-mastery of pain control to find help for his emotional problems. The man had suffered his first nervous breakdown twenty years before and had had subsequent seizures ever since, resulting in three breakdowns all together. He complained that before he tried self-mastery he had never been emotionally healthy.

"I have faithfully followed your directions," Thomas told me. "At the present time, I am able to take naps for a few minutes and wake up completely refreshed. Sunday I watched two football games on television, and my eyes became tired. I followed your directions. Within ten minutes my eyes were refreshed. I can't tell you how much your directions have helped me in other ways."

Recently Komar received a telephone call from a schoolteacher in West Virginia who said that Komar's methods had at last put the man's health matters into a proper perspective, and that he was getting tremendous results from using Komar's techniques.

A woman in Canton, Ohio, who suffered migraine headaches, attended classes and reported that she began receiving almost immediate relief.

According to Komar:

I do not personally heal people. I can only describe my techniques of pain control. I can only describe what I have done to unite my own mind and body, and what others should be able to do.

I am neither a holy man nor a superman, but one who has learned simple techniques for circumventing pain.

I believe that once one gains such mind and body control it is not difficult to eliminate a particular pain, ache, discomfort, tension, or ailment. Even some cases of cancer have been cured by using the mind.

I have not gleaned this information from books, but from the basic essences which I have isolated by working with human life. Throughout my lifetime I have been exposed to many people, and I have studied them. I have seen the aches, miseries, and pains of men and women. I have understood that what everyone is trying to do is to master the ultimate step where body and mind will be aligned. It is through this union that pain control is achieved.

In my first two steps toward self-mastery, you should learn to restructure your life toward a whole new area. You should make yourself emanate love, because you are learning what love is really all about.

A person who thinks negative thoughts creates an imbalance of hormones in the glandular system; and this causes aches, pains, misery, colds, flu, sickness of all sorts. We must restructure our lives to become positive, happy persons in order to achieve the ultimate and to be able to control ourselves through the steps of self-mastery.

Komar's Steps of Self-Mastery

The Power of Positive Attitude: You can't say, "I wish" or "I would like to." It must be, "I want; I will have." You must be very, very positive. You must become so strongly positive that you feel it within every fiber of the body.

Breathing: Complete and rhythmic breathing will bring you well along on the proper road toward self-mastery. I hope that I will not confuse you if I speak of *Prana*, as the yogis do. When the yogis breathe, they say they are breathing in Prana, the life-giving force.

Perhaps for our Western minds, if we substitute "electricity" for "Prana," we will get basically the same idea.

As you breathe in and do the Yoga breathing exercises, you build up a charge, a very strong electrical charge, along the spine. The spine actually becomes like a big capacitor.

As the charge builds up and you want to emit energy, you are able to change your electromagnetic field, which enables you to heal yourself.

When a healer lays hands upon another, he is releasing the charge that's been built up in his capacitor. Through the emission of electrical impulses from his healing hands, he is able to change the other person's electromagnetic field, causing him, in essence, to heal himself through the stimulus of the healer.

Relaxation: Relaxation emphasizes that you must tone the body, as well as the mind, and get them both into proper functioning order. It takes a very positive attitude to continue. It takes commitment; it takes discipline. But it is important to engage in exercise and to improve the circulation of the blood.

Concentration-Contemplation-Meditation: The active state of meditation, which I will call contemplation, is comparable to your state of mind just before you fall asleep. If you want to eliminate aches and pains, it will be at this level of contemplation, or active meditation, that you will do it. It is at this point where you will begin to program yourself to the state where you will be able to get rid of pains and whatever else might be troubling you. *It is in this state of mind that you can visualize perfect health, happiness, vitality, and no pain!*

You can program into your superconscious a conviction that you are capable of doing whatever you wish—even to conquer pain. Programming is essential, and I believe the contemplative state is the one in which to obtain this level of consciousness, just prior to advancing into the total, passive state of meditation.

But you must not confuse yourself. You must be very certain. You must analyze the cause of your pain. You must seek a doctor before you try to control a pain about which you know nothing.

A headache can be caused by a brain tumor, and I do not want anyone stifling a pain from a tumor instead of seeking medical help!

There are so many ways that pain can strike. Pain does not have to affect the specific part of the body from which it seems to be emanating. The pain may be coming from somewhere totally different than it seems.

Again, I repeat, *check with your medical doctor before undergoing this, or any other program of pain control.*

Five-Day Pain-Control Program

First Day

The First Five-Minute Session: Sit comfortably in a chair. Your back should be straight. Your legs should not be crossed; your feet should be flat on the floor.

As you breathe in, mentally state the words, "I feel..." As you breathe out, mentally state the words, "...no pain."

Your respiration should be natural and unforced as you repeat: "I feel...no pain. I feel...no pain."

This simple exercise is both a mental and a physical technique which relaxes the body, regulates respiration, and mentally conditions you to eliminate pain from your thinking processes. Continue this exercise for about three minutes.

Remain seated and proceed to the second technique in your first five-minute period of pain-control conditioning.

This exercise, the head roll, will loosen up the muscles, arteries, and veins of the neck and shoulders, all of which effect the ears, eyes, throat, and other organs of the body.

Sit up straight. Drop your head forward onto your chest. Without lifting your head, roll it to the left, up and over the left shoulder and over the back as far as possible.

After rolling your head to the left a few times, reverse and roll it to the right. Make as many complete circles as possible. Repeat this exercise for approximately two minutes.

If you should begin to experience a slight dizziness, cease the exercise and finish the two-minute time period with repetitions of "I feel...no pain."

The Second Five-Minute Session: Begin with two minutes of the head roll.

Conclude with three minutes of rhythmically breathing "I feel...no pain."

You have now begun and ended the first day of your program with the positive affirmation that you will not permit pain in your life.

Your very act of breathing—the physical action that most

assures one of being alive—has aided you in making this declaration of independence from unnecessary pain.

Second Day

The First Five-Minute Session: Stand up straight with your heels quite close together. Raise up on your toes, hold for a count of three, then lower yourself back done on your heels. This exercise is a good overall toner for the legs.

If an injury should somehow prevent you from performing the heel raise, sit up straight and flex your calf and thigh muscles for a three-second count.

The heel raise should be performed for approximately one minute.

Follow the heel raise with about two minutes of head rolls.

Complete your first five-minute session of the second day with two minutes of rhythmically breathing, "I feel...no pain."

The Second Five-Minute Session: Begin this session with a simple stretching exercise. Stand erect, feet comfortably apart. Raise your arms over your head and stretch for the ceiling.

Imagine your arms actually growing and reaching the light fixture.

Visualize your palms flattening against the ceiling. Even if an injury should prevent your standing erect, you may remain seated and still reach for the ceiling.

When tension in your arms becomes uncomfortable, lower them for a few seconds, then stretch once again.

This simple stretching exercise will help remove pressure against the vertebrae which may be pressing against certain nerves and causing pain. Continue this technique for two minutes.

Follow the stretching exercise with about one minute of head rolls to continue the relaxation of neck vertebrae.

Conclude this session with two minutes of rhythmically breathing, "I feel...no pain."

Third Day

The First Five-Minute Session: Begin with one minute of stretching.

Follow with one minute of heel raises.

Conclude with one minute of head rolls, two minutes of rhythmically breathing, "I feel...no pain."

The Second Five-Minute Session : Lie flat on the floor. For one minute, rhythmically breathe, "I feel...no pain." While continuing to breathe rhythmically, focus on the area of your body that is causing you pain.

Visualize the painful area as being colored a bright red. Imagine that you have a cool, damp cloth in your hand and begin to rub away the area of pain.

As the area becomes smaller and smaller, visualize the pain disintegrating, leaving you forever.

Conclude this session by rhythmically breathing, "I feel...no pain."

Fourth Day

The First Five-Minute Session: Begin this session by standing erect, raising your arms over your head, then bending at the waist to touch your toes. Do not despair if you cannot reach your toes. It is the effort and the stretching that is important.

If it is impossible to perform this exercise, either stand or sit erect and contract your stomach muscles as best you can for a count of three. Continue this exercise for one minute.

Rest for a moment, then proceed with one minute of stretching for the ceiling, one minute of head rolls.

Rest for a bit between those exercises and the concluding technique, which today is to perform one minute of heel raises closely followed by one minute of rhythmically breathing, "I feel...no pain."

The Second Five-Minute Session: Stand before a mirror and concentrate on your face.

While rhythmically breathing, "I feel...no pain," permit your face to assume a happier and happier expression.

Visualize the pain leaving your body as your smile becomes wider and more reflective of good health. Continue for the full five-minute session.

Fifth Day

The First Five-Minute Session: Begin the session by standing erect before a chair. Bend your knees until your buttocks touch the seat of the chair. Do not drop lower, but raise to a standing position at once. Repeat knee bends for one minute.

Continue by touching your toes for one minute, stretching for the ceiling for one minute, doing head rolls for one minute.

Rest for only a moment, then conclude with heel raises. This time, however, mentally recite, "I feel..." as you lift upward on your toes,"...no pain," as you lower to your heels. Repeat for one minute.

The Second Five-Minute Session: Stand before a mirror and mentally appraise yourself. Notice how much more relaxed your face appears. Take a moment to assess how much better your body feels. Pain is becoming a stranger to your life.

While still focusing on your smiling, healthy face, rhythmically breathe in forceful, joyful affirmation: "I feel...no pain!" Continue for the full five-minute session.

20

Sherry's Loving Touch

Sherry Hansen Steiger is a licensed massage therapist. She lists the following benefits of massage:

1. Relaxation that is equal to several hours of sleep, thereby reducing tension and the possibility of heart disease.
2. Improved circulation which improves the action of the heart and promotes general good health.
3. Improved digestion and the stimulation of the function of the skin, lungs, and kidneys.
4. Relieving the body of aches and pains, thus accelerating recuperation from injuries.
5. The activation of the skin glands, thus preventing the skin from aging.
6. The reduction of fat cells and the breaking down of fatty tissues.

"Massage results in a more youthful appearance, in better health, and allows the individual to feel better," Sherry says. "Contrary to myth, massage is a healing art, not an advanced sexual technique. Stress is one of today's most significant health problems. Massage not only helps one to unwind and to relax tightened muscles, but it promotes healthful circulation while toning the skin.

"Massage frees blocked energy in the human body," she continues. "It realigns muscular and connective tissue and brings about a greater sense of well being. I am convinced that healing takes place most effectively when energy is transmitted through the body while stress is being massaged away from the muscles."

A Miraculous Cure through Massage

Sherry relates the following miraculous cure which she effected through the use of massage. In this particularly dramatic case, a young woman named Carrie was left a quadriplegic after she had been terribly beaten. She had been flown to the finest military hospitals and discharged as "hopeless."

To complicate her case, during an exploratory brain surgery a portion of her motor brain had been "accidentally removed." She didn't even know her own mother. She was a vegetable.

The mother was told to put her in an institution. Not being able to bear this, the mother made arrangements for the daughter to be placed in a nursing home. On weekends Carrie was brought home to the farm in her wheelchair, so she could be with her family...where all hoped she could feel their love.

"My ex-husband and I would join them often," Sherry said, "Once while he was playing the guitar, and we were all sitting around singing together, I noticed something—a glimmer in Carrie's eyes. I mentioned it and everyone said...impossible. She can't respond.

"Well, in my heart I felt a connection and got a message. I asked for permission to start working with Carrie on weekends. I followed my intuitive guidance and did things totally and completely out of my character at that time."

When she was a nurse, Sherry had noticed how touch and love and caring immediately affected her patients' healing, but she had been extremely sensitive to their pain.

Even to move patients, if it hurt them, would cause her pain, too.

In Carrie's case, Sherry's inner guidance instructed her to massage the girl's mangled, twisted arms. "They were rigid and twisted up around her neck. I massaged and massaged them until I could force her arms down on the arms of the wheelchair...then I tied them to the chair," Sherry recalled. "Carrie would moan and carry on, but the whole time I'd be telling her that she'd be healed and that we loved her."

After many, many months of this process and Sherry's guiding her through self-relaxation on a cassette tape that the nurses played for her, Carrie said her first word: No!

"Eventually I got her to move her arm from the tied position on the wheelchair to her mouth with a tootsie pop," Sherry said. "Then I asked her mom to fix some mashed potatoes, and I worked with her to feed herself a spoonful.

"All of this took much time and effort, but most of all, a belief that it would work.

"I got the mother to call Craig Rehabilitation Hospital and tell them of the developments. We wanted an appointment for Carrie.

"They said it was totally impossible that Carrie could be doing any of the things that we said. But after much insistence, they made an appointment.

"In amazement, the rehabilitation hospital made arrangements and admitted Carrie.

"She underwent intensive therapies, and years later she had full use of her arms and hands," Sherry explained. "She also talked and interacted normally with others. There is even a chance she'll eventually be able to walk!"

"Everything here, but the soul of man, is a passing shadow. The only enduring substance is within. When shall we awake to the sublime greatness, the perils, the accountableness, and the glorious destinies of the immortal soul?"

William Ellery Channing

21

The Dancing Amerindian Healers

After he completed his medical internship in 1965, Dr. Carl Hammerschlag entered the Indian Health Service. He was sent to Santa Fe, N. M., as a general medical officer assigned to the Pueblo tribes along the Rio Grande River.

The twenty-six-year-old doctor knew nothing of Indians except what he'd seen in the movies. A city boy from New York, he thought "you needed to be immunized against yellow fever if you crossed the George Washington Bridge."

Today, in 1988, he understands that if you, as the doctor, believe that you are the only one who is involved in the healing process, you are setting yourself up for pain and disillusionment. But, in 1965, he had not viewed the connections of spirit that are involved in the process of healing. For Hammerschlag to begin to understand that, and thereby transform himself into a healer, he had to meet a Santo Domingo medicine man called Santiago.

Hammerschlag knew that Santiago, who was lying among other patients in a twenty-five-bed ward, was a traditional Indian priest and a clan chief. But at the time of their first meeting, the doctor saw him only as a man in his seventies with oxygen tubes up his nostrils.

The doctor responded to the patient's warm smile, but then he was taken aback when the priest asked him where he had learned to heal. Mildly annoyed, Hammerschlag rattled off his academic credentials, his place of medical internship, his certifications.

"But," the old man said with a beatific smile, "do you know how to dance?"

Did he know how to dance? He had to be Fred Astaire to remove an appendix?

Touched by Santiago's seemingly irrelevant query, the doctor put down his clipboard and shuffled a few dance steps at bedside.

Santiago began to laugh. He crawled out of bed and proceeded to show the doctor his own dance. "If you are to heal people," the priest told him, "you must be able to dance. I can teach you my steps, but you will have to hear your own music."

At that point in his evolution as a healer, Hammerschlag dismissed Santiago as another mystical holy man, and, only momentarily amused, continued his rounds. But Santiago had planted a seed.

Hammerschlag has come to see clearly that those men and women who best survive crises are those who have established a positive identity, a special sense of who they are. "If you are coming to greet the world as an equal, your feet have to be planted firmly in some unique, prideful recognition of Self," Hammerschlag says. "You must learn in a good way that what you are is okay. You must, in a positive way, become self-important.

"We are here to help each other discover our own individual uniqueness that will of itself sustain us and connect us to a larger reality of human and spiritual experience."

In 1970, Hammerschlag joined the Indian Health Service in Phoenix.

"I came to realize how much I had identified with the Indians' struggle," he says. "I perceive Indians as survivors. My parents and been survivors. They had seen the handwriting on the wall in 1936, and they had left Germany for America. I was born a few years after their immigration."

Hammerschlag is pleased that young Indians are coming back to their spiritual traditions by learning their languages and songs. "The watchword of our civilization has been to be independent, self-steering, goal-directed," he says, "but sometimes we feel weak. Sometimes we feel human. We need to be connected in those times. We need to know that we are connected to those who came before and to those who will come after us."

In the final analysis, he admits, the crises of modern life are not better alleviated by orthodox psychiatrists than by visionaries, "for both provide explanations for questions that have not simple answers."

Hammerschlag has come to see an inseparability between healing and a sense of the mystical. All rituals, all sacraments, beliefs, are methods of preparing us for the inevitable that bad things eventually happen to all of us. "Healing is a powerful, culturally endorsed ritual," he says. "There is no doubt that if you trust the practitioner and if you share the same cultural myths, healing is better achieved."

To better complete the curative process in the Indian community he serves, Hammerschlag openly observes the burning of sweet grass and cedar. "Indians look to the heart of the doctor to decide whether or not to come to him," he says. "The doctor must convince them that he has the power to heal. To accomplish this, the doctor must learn to change the ordinary to the sacred. Corn pollen, sweet grass, incense, rosaries, prayer shawls—they all help us to separate the sacred from the profane.

"If I, as a doctor, cure someone, aid him to become less vulnerable to that disease and help him at the same time to understand his place in the universe, then I am a healer.

"The power to heal comes from hearing your own music and dancing your own dance."

Making the Ordinary Sacred

Hammerschlag greatly admires the work of Milton Erickson, the master hypnotherapist who died in Phoenix in 1980. "His basic tools were always whatever the patient gave him," Hammerschlag says. "Erickson firmly believed that the doctor and the patient must share the same language, the same symbols, and that they must together trust the unconscious.

"Erickson told us that we have to use all of our healing skills if we want to do the work well. He would use secret words, fetishes, masks, dolls. He would even send patients on pilgrimages.

"Like a skilled medicine man, Erickson was a genius at helping his patients to maintain their own genuine, true connection to their centers. He had found the truth that I had also discovered from working with the Indian healers: *You* are the connection. You can make your ordinary experiences sacred so that you can separate them from the mundane.

"All the great healers whom I have met have enabled their people to build bridges over the unknowable gaps, the mysteries of our existence." Hammerschlag says. "As doctors, we must never denigrate the great technological advances that we have made in medicine, but we must not lose sight of the Big Picture. Science is too reductionistic. It keeps forgetting that the small parts always add up to more than their sum."

No One Makes It Alone

Hammerschlag would be terribly saddened if the cynical were to interpret his enthusiasm for the effectiveness of Indian healing techniques as that of another big-city psychiatrist who put on the moccasins and embraced the romantic myths of earlier cultures. "I do not want anyone to rush to the reservations and attempt to walk the Indians' walk," he says. "I certainly do not want them to insist upon walking my walk.

"We must all learn to feel how other people connect to one another and to the universe. No one makes it alone. We must all be connected to something other than ourselves.

"And, at the same time, we are unique. We all have our own truths and our own power, and it is these which we must follow."

22

Vision Quest for Spiritual Transformation

In the Native American Indian philosophy of Medicine Power, the vision quest is more than a goal received. It marks the beginning of a life-long search for wisdom and knowledge. In numerous seminars I have spoken of my admiration for the discipline and commitment practiced by the true and/or traditional adherents of the way of Medicine.

In the course of my own personal quest, I have spent a great deal of time with Medicine People from many different tribes in the United States. In my book *Indian Medicine Power* I put together what I believe to be the most essential elements of that spiritual construct. I realize how presumptuous it is to try to distill into eight steps the very essence of the cosmology of the many different tribes; but it is my opinion that, in spite of the great cultural differences I found from tribe to tribe, I seemed to notice the same basic elements of spiritual expression. I have broken those elements down this way:

1. The vision quest with its emphasis on self-denial and the spiritual discipline which is extended to a life-long pursuit of wisdom of body and soul.
2. A reliance upon one's personal visions and individual dreams to provide one's direction on the path of life.

3. A search for personal songs to enable one to become attuned to the primal sounds, the cosmic vibration of the great spirit.

4. A belief in a total partnership with the world of spirits and in the ability to make a personal contact with grandfathers and grandmothers who have changed planes of existence.

5. The possession of a nonlinear time sense.

6. A receptivity toward the evidence that the essence of the Great Spirit may be found in everything.

7. A reverence and a passion for the Earth Mother, the awareness of one's place in the web of life, and one's responsibility toward all plant and animal life.

8. A total commitment to one's beliefs that evades every aspect of one's total life and enables one truly to walk in balance.

For a number of years, I have incorporated my own personal cosmology with American Indian Medicine Power. I find that it is imperative in Native American magic or in any practice of metaphysics to set a time apart to enter the Silence.

A Condensed Daily Vision Quest

In a sense, I do a condensed version of the vision quest every day. I have a daily exercise routine in which I work vigorously with barbells and dumbells, ride a bicycle, and go for a long walk in order to exert my body and distract my conscious self. I find that just as a person on a vision quest may deplete the physical self through monotonous and strenuous tasks in order to free the subconscious, the workout with weights accomplishes this same goal for me.

After my period of exercise, I enter a hot shower (which is my counterpart of a sweat lodge). After I have towel-dried, I lie flat on my back in a quiet place, apart from everyone and all distractions, and permit whatever is to come to me from the Silence easy access to my heightened state of awareness.

For added physical stimulus, I might wrap myself in a blanket, covering even my head. Such a withdrawal and sealing off of self increases my sensation of being totally isolated and permits me to become even less aware of my physical body and my surroundings.

The Medicine Bag

Traditional Medicine people carry a medicine bag which is filled with objects regarded as personally sacred to the bearer. If you should try to emulate this practice, remember to include objects symbolic of the four elements—fire, water, air, and earth. Remember, too, that these objects (and any other items that may have personal significance to you) serve as physical stimuli upon which you might meditate in order to open the channel of your subconscious.

You may wish to go out, as many Native Americans do, to find your medicine stone. The medicine stone is something you can carry in your bag. Or, you might choose to drill a hole through it and wear it about your neck on a leather thong, as a kind of physical stimulus.

The Personal Song

During the vision quest, one often acquires a personal song or sound. This personal vibration will greatly facilitate you in future meditation. If you have not already received such a song or sound, don't overlook certain pieces of music, which may contain nostalgic triggers that will work for you, invoking images of great strength.

Nearly everyone has a song that is loaded with particularly sentimental images. Sometimes those melodies can send you back to a special experience. And then, after that moment has been relived, your unconscious can soar here and there, often returning with valuable insights.

Music can take you into the past, then allow you to daydream or wander mentally into areas where your higher self can reach down and bring you up by the hand into greater awarenesses. Listening to music is an ideal way to "prime the pump," to get your creative and meditative mechanisms into full operation.

Do not neglect the many fine recordings of Native American music. Some recent New Age compositions combine the traditional with modern recording techniques. Two contemporary composer-artists, whose work is particularly effective in helping me to transcend the ordinary world, are Steven Halpern and Iasos.

A Partnership with the Spiritual World

In our modern American society, some people may be uneasy about stating a belief in a total partnership with the world of spirits. I suggest that you at least keep the door open to the possibility that you may be able to establish contact with those who have graduated to other planes of existence.

Under no circumstances should the situation be forced. A relaxed and tranquil state of mind will best permit your psyche to soar free of time and space and return with images, impressions, and messages.

Accepting a Non-Linear Time Frame

One of the most difficult things for modern man or woman practicing American Indian Medicine to learn is to live in a nonlinear time sense. Our society is so completely and lavishly governed by the human-made markings of linear time, that we must, through meditation, stop the world and learn how to develop a magic or spiral time sense.

As I have stated repeatedly, meditation affords the most effective method I know for allowing us to break free of the boundaries of conventional time. We must always realize that central to an understanding of any system of metaphysics is the knowledge that, for one level of the unconscious (the deepest and most spiritually attuned level), linear time does not exist. All is an Eternal Now. An altered-state-of-consciousness properly conducted will permit you to enter that time-free, unchartered, measureless kingdom of the psyche.

Responsibility to the Web of Life

At the same time, you must establish a close connection to the Earth Mother, and learn to really see and appreciate all of her adornments and trappings.

You must come to know that you are a part of the universe and that the universe is a part of you. You must recognize that the essence of the Great Spirit is to be found in all things—and all things are as yet too subtle for your total comprehension.

You must bear your responsibility toward all plant and animal life with dignity and not with condescension. In my opinion, a total commitment to such Medicine Power is in complete harmony with the basic belief structures of all schools of positive metaphysical teachings, and should be considered complimentary to those bodies or philosophical thoughts which we call orthodox religions.

Embarking on Your Vision Quest

Here is a guided meditation that I have used at vision quests and Medicine Wheel gatherings throughout the United States and Canada. It is one that I have found very effective for guiding men and women into a simulated vision quest experience. You can pre-record this in your voice and become your own guide through the experience. Or, you may read it aloud to a trusted friend or loved one, and then have that same individual read it for you to lead you through the experience.

Enter a state where your mind is very relaxed, either through a yogic breathing technique, color visualization, or one of the other techniques that I have shared with you in earlier chapters.

When you have reached a deep level, when you have gone deep, deep, within—moving toward the very center of your essence—begin to tell yourself that you have the ability to visualize in your mind the conditions of your vision quest. Tell yourself that you have the ability to tap into the eternal transmission of universal truth from which you may draw power and strength. You have the ability to evolve as a spiritual being.

Visualize yourself as a Native American man or woman on a vision quest.

Focus your thoughts on your performance of some mundane, monotonous physical task. Perhaps like so many young Native American men and women on a vision quest, you have found a small clearing in the forest which has a number of rocks of various sizes at one end of the nearly barren area. Pick up one of the rocks and carry it to the opposite side of the clearing. In your mind, see yourself carrying the rock. See yourself placing the rock down on the ground and turning around to get another rock. See yourself picking up a new rock, carrying it slowly to the other side of the clearing, and then another rock, and another, back and forth. Back and forth, over and over again.

Know and understand that you are performing this task for the sole purpose of depleting the physical self with monotonous exercise. Know and understand that you are distracting the unconscious mind with dull activity, that you are doing this to free the essential self within you, so that it can soar free of the physical body.

Feel your body becoming very, very tired. Your body is feeling very heavy. It feels very, very dull. You have no aching muscles or sore tendons, but you are very, very tired. Your physical body is exhausted. See yourself lying down on the blanket to rest, to relax.

Slowly you become aware of a presence. Someone has approached you and has come to stand next to you. As you look up at the figure, you see that it is a most impressive individual. It is a man who is looking at you with warmth and compassion.

And now you notice that he has been joined by a woman who is equally impressive, almost majestic in appearance. She smiles at you, and you feel as if she stands before that you are enveloped in the Great Mother vibration.

Before you can open your mouth to speak, the man and the woman fade from your sight. They simply disappear.

You realize that they were spirits, that they came to you from the spirit world to demonstrate to you that, in many ways, on many levels, you have a subtle, yet intense, partnership with the world of the spirits. The spirit man and spirit woman have given you a visual sign of the reality of this oneness with all spiritual forms of life.

You have but a moment to ponder the significance of the spirit visitation when you become aware of two globes of bluish-white light moving toward you. You are not afraid, for you sense a great spiritual presence approaching you.

As you watch in great expectation, the first glow of bluish-white light begins to assume human form. As the light swirls and becomes solid, you behold before you a man or a woman whom you regard as a holy person, a saint, a master, an illumined one.

This figure, so beloved to you, gestures to your left side. As you turn, you are astonished to see a marvelous link-up with other holy figures from all times, from all places, from all cultures. You see that these personages form a beautiful spiritual chain from prehistory to the present—and without doubt, the future.

The holy one smiles benevolently, then bends over you and touches your shoulder gently. The holy one's forefinger lightly touches your eyes, your ears, then your mouth.

You know within that this touching symbolizes that you are about to see and to hear a wondrous revelation, which you must share with others.

As the holy figure begins to fade from your perception, the second globe of bluish-white light begins to materialize into human form.

The entity that forms before you now may be very familiar to you. You may have seen this entity in your dreams, for this is your guide—one who has always loved you just as you are. This guide has unconditional love for you and is concerned completely with your spiritual evolution. You feel totally relaxed, at peace, at one with your guide. You feel totally loved.

Your guide is now showing you something important. Your guide's hands are holding something for you to see. It is an object which you can clearly identify, an object which will serve as a symbol that you are about to receive a meaningful and important teaching in your dreams. Whenever you see this symbol in your dreams, you will understand that an important and significant teaching will instantly follow.

The symbol fades from your sight, but you will remember it.

Now, in a great rush of color and light, you are finding yourself elevated in spirit. You know that your guide has taken you to a higher vibrational level. You have moved to a dimension where nonlinear, cyclical time flows around you.

From your previous limited perspective of Earth time, linear time, you are aware that you now exist in a timeless realm in an Eternal Now.

Stretching before you is something that appears to be a gigantic tapestry that has been woven of multi-colored living lights—lights that are pulsating, throbbing with life. The energy of the Great Spirit touches your inner knowing, and you are made aware that you are becoming one with the great pattern of all life.

In a marvelous, pulsating movement of beautiful lights and living energy, your soul feels a unity with all living things.

You see before you now an *animal*, any animal.

You become one with its essence.

You become one with this level of awareness. Be that animal.

Be that level of energy expression.

See before you a *bird,* any bird.
Now become one with its essence.
Become one with its level of awareness. Be that bird.
Be that level of energy expression.

See before you a *creature of the waters,* any creature.
Become one with its essence.
Become one with its level of awareness.
Be that marine creature.
Be that level of energy expression.

See before you an *insect,* any insect crawling or flying.
Become one with its essence.
Become one with its level of awareness.
Be that insect.
Be that level of energy expression.

See before you a *plant,* any flower, tree, grass, or shrub.
Become one with its essence.
Become one with its level of awareness.
Be that plant.
Be that level of energy expression.

Know now that you are one with the unity of all plant and animal essence. Know now that you forever bear responsibility to all plant and animal life. You are one with all things that walk on two legs or four, with all things that fly, with all things that crawl, with all things that grow in the soil or sustain themselves in the waters.

Listen carefully as your guide begins to tell you your secret name, your spirit name, the name that only you will know, that only you and your guide will share. It is the name by which your guide will contact you. Hear that name *now.*

And now your guide is showing you the image of an animal, a plant, a bird, a water creature, an image of one of the little brothers or sisters other than humankind. Focus upon that creature. See its beauty. Become one with its beauty.

Know that this animal, this creature, is now your *totem*--a symbol that will come to you often in dreams and represent the spirit of yourself on another level of reality.

See before you another person, a man, a woman, young or old.

Go into that person.

Become one with that person's essence.

Become one with that person's level of awareness.

Be that person.

Be that level of energy expression.

Know now that it is never yours to judge another expression of humankind. Know now that you have a common brotherhood and sisterhood with all of humankind.

Remember always that you must do unto your brothers and sisters as you would have them do to you. Remember always that the great error is to prevent in any way another's spiritual evolution.

At this eternal second in the energy of the Eternal Now, at this vibrational level of oneness with all living things, at this frequency of awareness of unity with the cosmos, your guide is permitting you to receive a great rush of healing energy that will balance your body, mind, and spirit. Receive this great healing energy.

You will awaken at the count of five, filled with memories of your great vision quest. When you awaken, you will feel morally elevated, you will feel intellectually illuminated. You will know that your spiritual essence is immortal. You will no longer fear death. You will no longer experience guilt or a sense of sin. You will feel filled with great charm and personal magnetism. You will feel better and healthier than ever before in your life, and you will feel a great sense of Unity with all living things. One, two, three, four, five—*awake*!

"It seems to me as if not only the form but the soul of man was made to walk erect and to look at the stars." *Bulwer*

23

A Miracle from the Madonna

A few years ago, a miracle occurred to Mary Ranahan. Without hesitation, she attributes the extraordinary event to the Virgin Mary.

Mary Ranahan's story is one of thousands throughout history —particularly noticeable since the beginning of the Christian Era—a story of a miracle. Such stories will continue to happen.

"I was dying from drug abuse, malnutrition, and a general fear of living," the Phoenix, Arizona woman told me. "I suffered from chronic migraines. I endured several *grand mal* seizures each month and managed to survive numerous smaller epileptic seizures during the same period of time.

"I weighed 250 pounds. I was a compulsive junk food eater. My principal food was cold cereal with several inches of sugar on top."

Doctors had told Mary that she had a brain tumor. But she was so fearful of life itself that such a dread diagnosis barely registered on her consciousness. She was so afraid of contact with human beings that she had been almost totally homebound for years.

On that day in June, Mary knew she *was* dying. She could no longer get out of bed. Her husband Bob had to help her to the bathroom.

"I knew that the time had come for me to die and go to hell," she recalled. "I knew that I was going to hell, for that was where bad people went—and I had always been told that I was bad. At the same time I was happy—death would mean that a lifetime of misery, fear, and hell-on-Earth would soon be over."

Bob asked her if she minded if he left the motel room in which they were living so that he might attend a meeting. She began to cry and begged him not to leave her. She felt so alone.

"Suddenly without warning, an explosion occurred both inside and outside my body," she recalled. "I was filled with a presence that I had never known before. *A great and beautiful aura descended all around me.*"

Mary was now convinced that she was dying. Slowly her consciousness left her body and she began to move away from the concerns of the world.

"I arose from my body—away from the motel room—away from Earth!"

Before she soared free of the motel room, she could see her husband, Bob, sitting at her bedside, probably assuming that she was asleep. She felt light, free—happy to leave the problems of the material plane far behind her.

The soul—the essential self of Mary Ranahan—moved upward through higher dimensions until she found herself in the august presence of a beautiful angel.

"She wore a light, pink robe and had very long, blonde hair," Mary stated as she squinted her eyes in an effort to focus on her recollection. "When I asked her who she was, she astonished me by replying that she was my own spirit! 'I am you, little one,' she told me. And as I looked at her face, I saw that it was my own."

The angel informed Mary that she had chosen a lifetime in which the first forty-eight years would be ones of great testing to determine if she would choose good over evil. Although Mary's life had been filled with terror, misery, and humiliation, the angel told her that she had succeeded in passing the period of testing. Not once had she been dishonest. Not once had she chosen evil over good.

Because she persevered, Mary was told that her purpose on Earth was not over. She must return to the body to receive a "beautiful and wonderful miracle."

Specifically, Mary was instructed and assured that during the next seven years of her life, seven angels would enter her body.

Her physical body would become slim once again. The headaches would no longer trouble her. The seizures would cease. Her pessimistic, terror-stricken thoughts would change.

She would become an extremely optimistic, positive-thinking person.

She would become young again—both in body and in spirit!

Mary said that she awakened back in her motel room. She reached out her hand, touched Bob and told him, "Go to your meeting, beloved husband, for I am no longer alone."

The old cravings and old compulsions were gone.

Her carton-a-day cigarette habit ceased completely.

She had no further need for drugs.

The headaches vanished.

The seizures became dreaded experiences of the past.

The once-diagnosed brain tumor mysteriously disappeared.

At the present time, in 1988, this fifty-five-year-old woman stands confidently before the world to tell of her miracle, to testify to the loving energy and the everlasting power of the Virgin Mary.

Mary Ranahan smiles easily. Her soft, sincere voice celebrates life. She appears youthful in her mannerisms, and the slimness of her body offers dramatic testimony that she has shed eighty-five pounds of fat.

"One of the angels of the Virgin Mary entered my brain and began to re-program me," she recalled. "The angel told me that no longer must I think of myself as human garbage.

"Another angel entered me soon after that and we began to speak back and forth. I understood the truth that you are what you think you are. If you accept the vicious programming of others that you are garbage, then you will act accordingly. If you think positive thoughts about yourself, then you will live as a true, victorious child of God."

Through channeling it was revealed that Mary Ranahan has become the human counterpart of the Virgin Mary. "The energy of the Virgin entered me and permits me to heal others. I now have the hands of the Holy Spirit so that I might give life to others."

Mary Ranahan states firmly that she does not believe that she was born again so that she might seek self-glorification. "I am here only to help people. I wish to reach as many people as possible with my story, and it is not my intention to offend anyone with the truth of my experience.

"I want people to be able to use in their own lives whatever elements of my story speak to them.

"The Virgin Mary speaks to us all in her own special way, and her knowledge, light, and compassion flows out into the world through us."

24

Time Travelling with Master Healers

"Life is the soul's nursery—its training place for the destinies of eternity." *Thackeray*

Relax. Visualize the color blue moving over your body as if it were a blanket-like aura. Feel it moving over your feet, soothing them. Feel it moving over your legs, relaxing them. Feel it moving over your stomach, your chest, your arms, your neck—soothing them, relaxing them.

Now as you make a hood of the blue-colored auric cover, feel the color blue permeating your psyche, activating it to use the power of Universal Love for clairvoyance, prophecy, and healing. Once you have done this, visualize yourself bringing the blue-colored aura over your head. You are now sitting or lying totally secure in your blue-colored auric cover.

You are very receptive, very aware. You feel attuned with Higher Consciousness. You feel prepared to explore deep, deep within you; deep, deep within you...as awareness grows within you.

You are seeing memory patterns before you. They may be your memories of a past-life experience. They may be the memories of another. It does not matter. You are seeing them before you now.

The memories are taking you to a faraway place in a faraway time. You are moving back on the vibration of the Eternal Now. You are moving back in time to the Egypt of the second century before the birth of the Master Jesus. You are remembering that you heard scholars tell of an ancient manuscript which was found in a column of an Egyptian temple. You heard a scholar say that this book told of miracle healings which occurred at the beginning of Time when Great Beings communicated secrets to initiated adepts.

You have heard it said that this incredible, ancient revelation is being taught in secret to a few select adepts in hidden rooms in the pyramids. The objects of these teachings are health and longevity, the manipulation of physical matter, and the production of the elixir of immortality.

See yourself now walking a street in the Egypt of that time. There is a full Moon, and you can see everything around you very clearly. You are approaching a home with a courtyard. It is the home of a very old and wise teacher who can lead you to a secret room in a pyramid and who can give you the initiation which will make you a master healer.

Take a moment to experience fully your emotions as you walk up the path to the home. Feel deeply your expectations. What plants grow near the walls? What is there about the immediate area that most captures your attention?

Now you are at the front gate. Be aware of your inner thoughts and feelings as you knock. Feel your knuckles strike the wooden planks.

The gates open as if by themselves, and you see the dancing flames of a great open fire that burns in the center of the courtyard. You are able to see a man dressed in robes sitting near the fire. You know it is the Master Healer. As you approach him a student steps forward and places more wood upon the fire. As the flames dance higher, you are able to see the Healer very clearly.

Become totally aware of him. See his clothes, his body, his face, his eyes, his mouth, the way he holds his hands.

You have brought a present for him so he might recognize you as a seeker of the art of healing. Take your present out of the leather bag in which you have carried it. See what it is that you hand the Master Healer. See his reaction to the gift.

The Healer gestures to you that you should follow him. He has approved of you as one who will receive initiation.

You are now in a tunnel. You are being led to a secret room within one of the great pyramids. Experience fully your emotions as you walk silently through the tunnel. Feel deeply your expectations. See the torches set into the walls. Be aware of any aromas, any sounds.

Now you are in a great room. Look around you slowly. You see statues, golden statues.

Look at the walls, see the paintings. See the hieroglyphics.

The Healer is showing you a great crystal that is supported on a golden tripod. He says that it is the Philosopher's Stone.

As you stare into the crystal, the Healer tells you that he will now bestow upon you the initiation. He says that it will be personal, completely customized for your particular needs. The Healer will tell you what you need to know from him. He will tell you what you need to know to continue your quest for healing.

Observe him closely. He may transmit his initiation with a facial expression alone. He may transmit this initiation with a gesture of the hands or a movement of the body. Or he may transmit this initiation at some length with carefully selected words. He might even show you an object or a symbol. However he transmits the knowledge, it will be for your good and your gaining. He is transmitting the initiation...NOW....

Whatever the Master Healer has told you, he has bestowed the gift of mastery of Cosmic Time and Human Time upon you. You are moving through the Purple Mists of Time to seek knowledge from another great master healer.

You have heard it said that there are certain great spiritual adepts who obtained the elixir of immortality and who became immortals, wandering for centuries upon Earth, concealing their condition of immortality and revealing themselves to only a few high-minded students. You are now approaching the forest cottage of such a being. He is one who has achieved enormous fame as a healer.

You are walking the forest trail without fear, for the healer has sent a knight in armor to guide you. It is late at night, but there is a full Moon, and the trail is easy to see in the moonlight.

As you approach the cottage, what do you most notice about the house and the outbuildings? Is there a garden? Do trees grow near the main building? Take a moment to know the healer's environment.

The healer whom you are seeking is said to be able to answer any question about the art of healing which might be put to him. You are pleased that you have received an invitation to visit this wise one. The knight walks you to the open door of the cottage, then steps aside so that you might enter alone.

As you enter the cottage, you see the crackling flames of a great open fireplace. Someone dressed in robes sits near the fire, stirring a huge iron kettle with a large wooden ladle. You know it is the healer.

As the healer turns to face you, you see his features clearly in the firelight. Become totally aware of him. See his clothes, his body, his face, his eyes, his mouth, the way he moves his hands.

He gestures to you that you should be seated. He hands you a cup of his favorite tea, and you savor it gratefully. Taste the tea in your mouth. It is very special herbal tea.

The healer nods to you, indicating that you may now ask your question about how you might best develop control of the healing power of love.

He will now answer what method will be best for you. Observe him closely. He may answer you with a facial expression alone. He may answer with a gesture of the body. He may answer you at some length with carefully selected words. He may show you some object or a symbol. However he answers, he will tell you what you need to know to develop your spiritual abilities for healing. However he answers, he will tell you what you need to know for your good and your gaining. He is answering the question...NOW...

The knight appears and tells you that you must now leave the healer. As you are saying goodbye, the ancient one reaches in his robe and brings forth a leather bag. He tells you that he has a very special gift for you to use in your healing work. He wants you to take the object with you. He opens the leather bag and hands you the gift. Look at it. See what it is. Take the gift. Feel it. Know it. Tell the healer how you feel about him and his gift.

Now the Purple Mist of Time is once again swirling around you, bringing you back to the present time. At the count of three, you will awaken feeling better than you have felt in weeks, filled with new insights into healing. One...two...three! Awaken!

25

You Can Create the Healing Power of Love

My wife, Sherry, is in strict agreement with Paramahansa Yogananda's admonition to place God first in each new day. As the great mystic phrased it in his work, *Man's Eternal Quest,* "First things must come first. When you awaken in the morning, meditate. If you don't, the whole world will crowd in to claim you, and you will forget God."

I must state that since I have begun following her example of beginning the day in such a manner, I have felt a sense of spiritual power and accomplishment previously unattained on my personal quest. Our process of bringing up the spiritual energy is to read from the Old Testament, the New Testament, Psalms, Proverbs, the Apocrypha, the Deutro-canonical texts, and from such enlightened masters as Yogananda. Our reading is followed with a discussion period that may last a few minutes—or as long as our schedules will permit.

Our prayer time is silent or aloud, again depending upon need, urgency, or the direction of Spirit. It is either at that time—or in the subsequent quiet time of meditation—that we ask for the healing of those who have requested such an extension of energy from us.

The operative word is "requested." As I have stated earlier in this text, it is unwise—perhaps even a violation of a person's free will—to transmit healing to anyone without that person's express permission.

Serving as a Conduit for the Holy Spirit

Throughout the centuries, certain inspired men and women have known that it is possible to serve as the medium, the conduit, for energy that issues from a Higher Intelligence to their own finite intelligence. This energy has been called the *chi*, the *mana*, the *prana*, the *Wakan*, the *Ruah*, the *Holy Spirit*, and it can be used to strengthen the soul, to heal the body, or to elevate consciousness. It is the essence of love, and it is the greatest power in the Universe.

Sherry and I believe that this energy can be sought through a program of regular meditation and a commitment to a self-disciplined lifestyle. Although there are some rare "Paul-on-the-road-to-Damascus" instances wherein a person receives an instantaneous illumination experience, the great majority of seekers receive the Holy Spirit through a life lived as an extended vision quest, ever vigilant to the snares and temptations of the dark side of the Force.

Healing with a Love Partner

Each of the exercises and techniques in this book can be employed by a single individual focusing his or her own love energy, but there is no question in my mind that the formula of "two or three gathering together" increases the power many times over.

If you work with a love partner, as I do with Sherry, then it is important that both individuals have come to believe that they can reshape the stuff of ordinary reality. In simplest terms, what I am saying is that you must believe that you *can* achieve such an experience as the manifestation of healing, and you must *affirm* that new reality with all of your will.

At the same time, you must affirm that you will seek to purify and to order your life—physically, emotionally, and mentally—so that you will do all that you can to make yourself a high-quality receiving set for the Holy Spirit. You must affirm that you will strive for balance in all facets of your life and that you will seek always to remain positive and well-grounded.

When you have entered seriously a regimen of self-discipline, prayer, and meditation, you must also understand completely that it is not enough to ask for a healing, you must affirm that the physical state that you desire *has already materialized.*

I urge that you conduct your healing work with a love partner—a spouse, a child, a dear friend, a sibling—for the following important reasons:

1. Together you can reach an agreement of the new reality of total health.
2. You can provide one another with important feedback of verification.
3. You can intensify one another's commitment to replace the former conventional interpretation of reality with the new construct of what is.
4. You can agree together to serve the new reality of complete health.
5. You can check one another so that the Love Force is not being subverted by the desires of the dark side.

Share the Healing Power of Love

Remember, whatever power you may receive from Spirit must in turn be surrendered to the Universe and immediately be supplanted with a desire to share the energy with others. Any attempt to focus the power of Spirit for unworthy goals will only destroy the channel that seeks to misuse it.

Again, I emphasize that your love partner can prove

invaluable for helping you to retain a delicate line of balance on the physical plane.

So, now it is up to you. You can heal; you can restructure your reality; you can recharge the negative with the positive. But to paraphrase St. Paul, "If you don't have love in your heart, you have nothing that will endure."

51295
9 780914 918844
ISBN 0-914918-84-2